GUYANA IS A MELTING POT OF MULTIPLE COLORS. THIS COLORING BOOK HIGHLIGHTS SOME OF GUYANA'S RICH HISTORY AND CULTURE.

BY : LEON LABASTIDE

GUYANA IN COLOR

Coloring Book

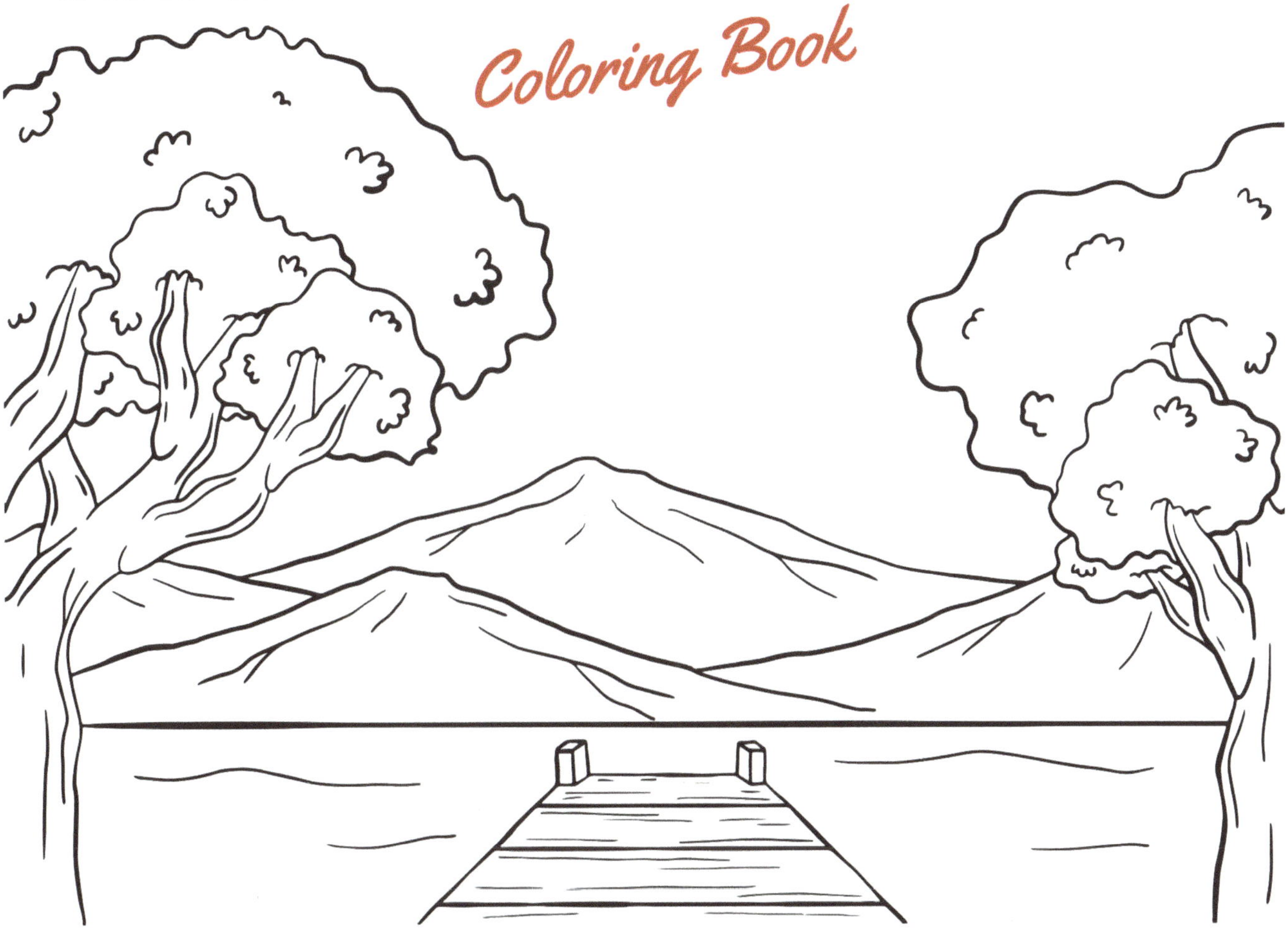

HIS COLORING BOOK WAS DESIGNED TO HIGHLIGHT SOME OF GUYANA'S LANDMARKS AND MONUMENTS IN A FEW OF OUR CELEBRITIES THAT IS PAVING THE WAY FOR THE FUTURE GENERATION OF GUYANESE.

BY : LEON LABASTIDE

A FEW OF THESE PAGES WAS ILLUSTRATED

BY LEVON LABASTIDE

THIS COLORING BOOK BELONGS TO

your name :

_____

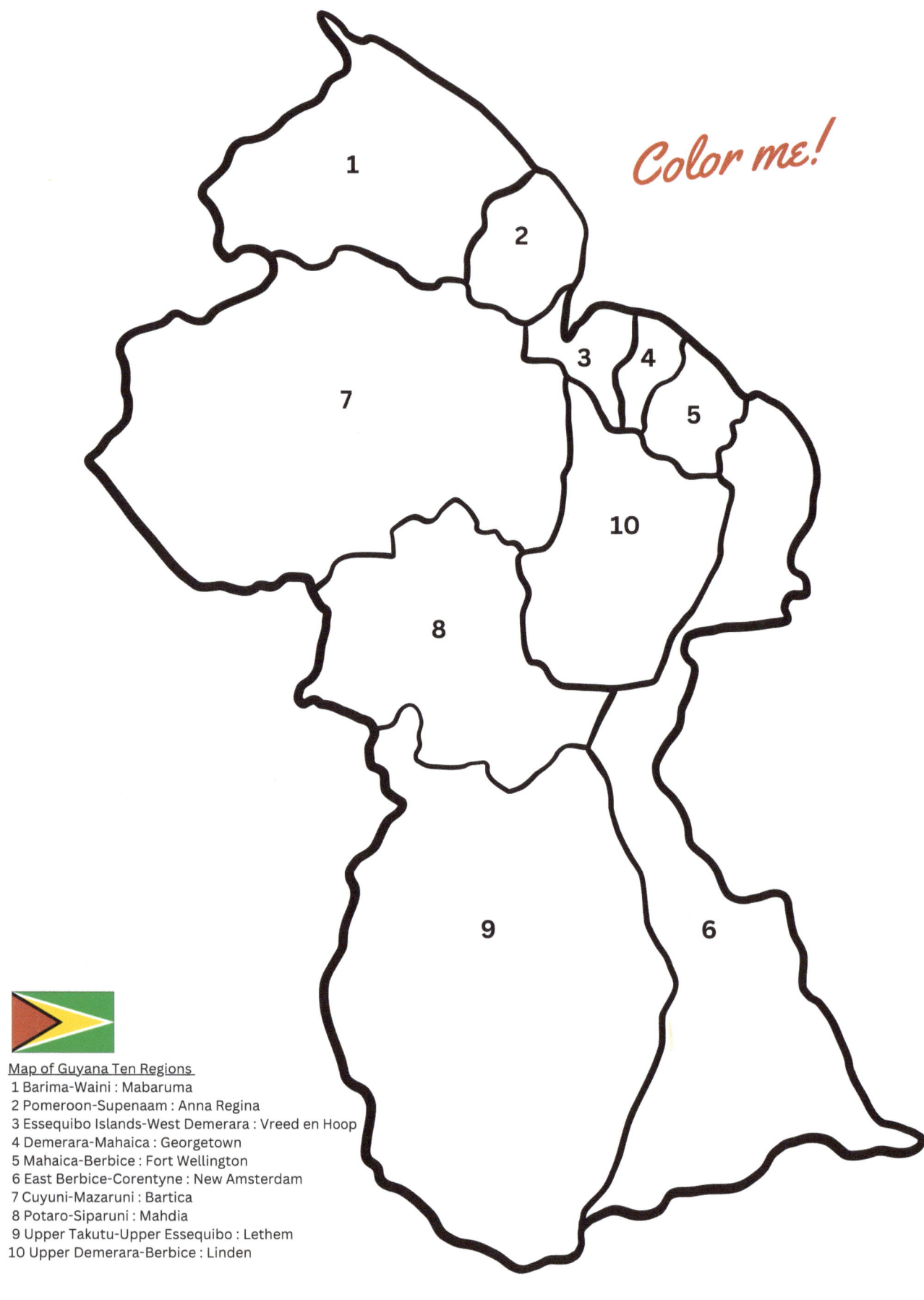

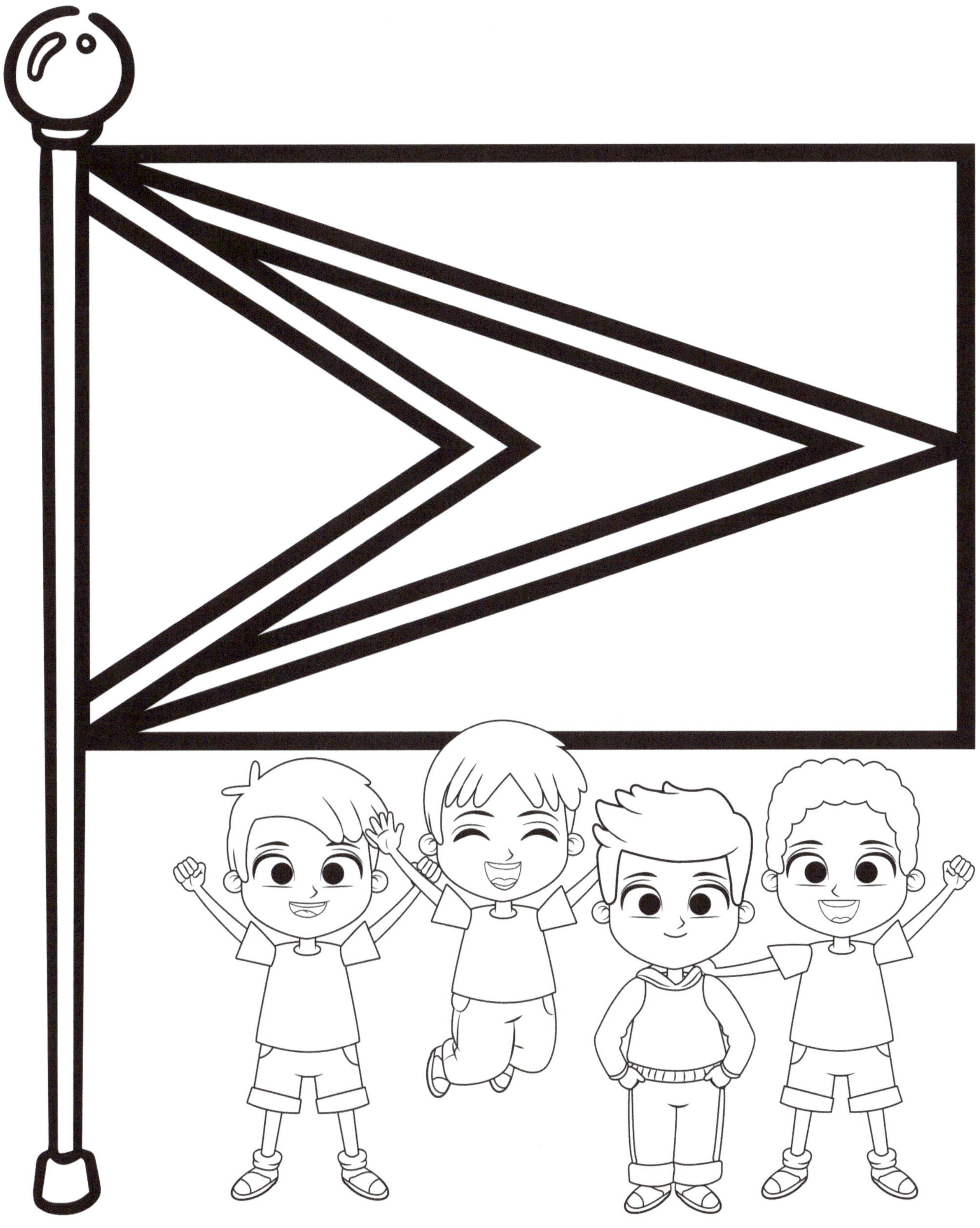

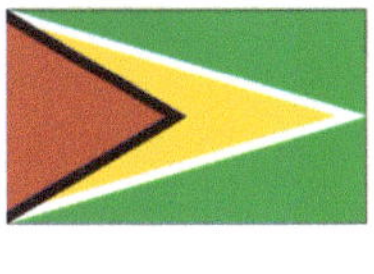

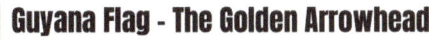

Guyana Flag - The Golden Arrowhead

has been the national flag of Guyana since May 1966 when the country became independent from the United Kingdom. **The colors are symbolic, with red for zeal and dynamism, gold for mineral wealth, green for agriculture and forests, black for endurance, and white for rivers and water.**

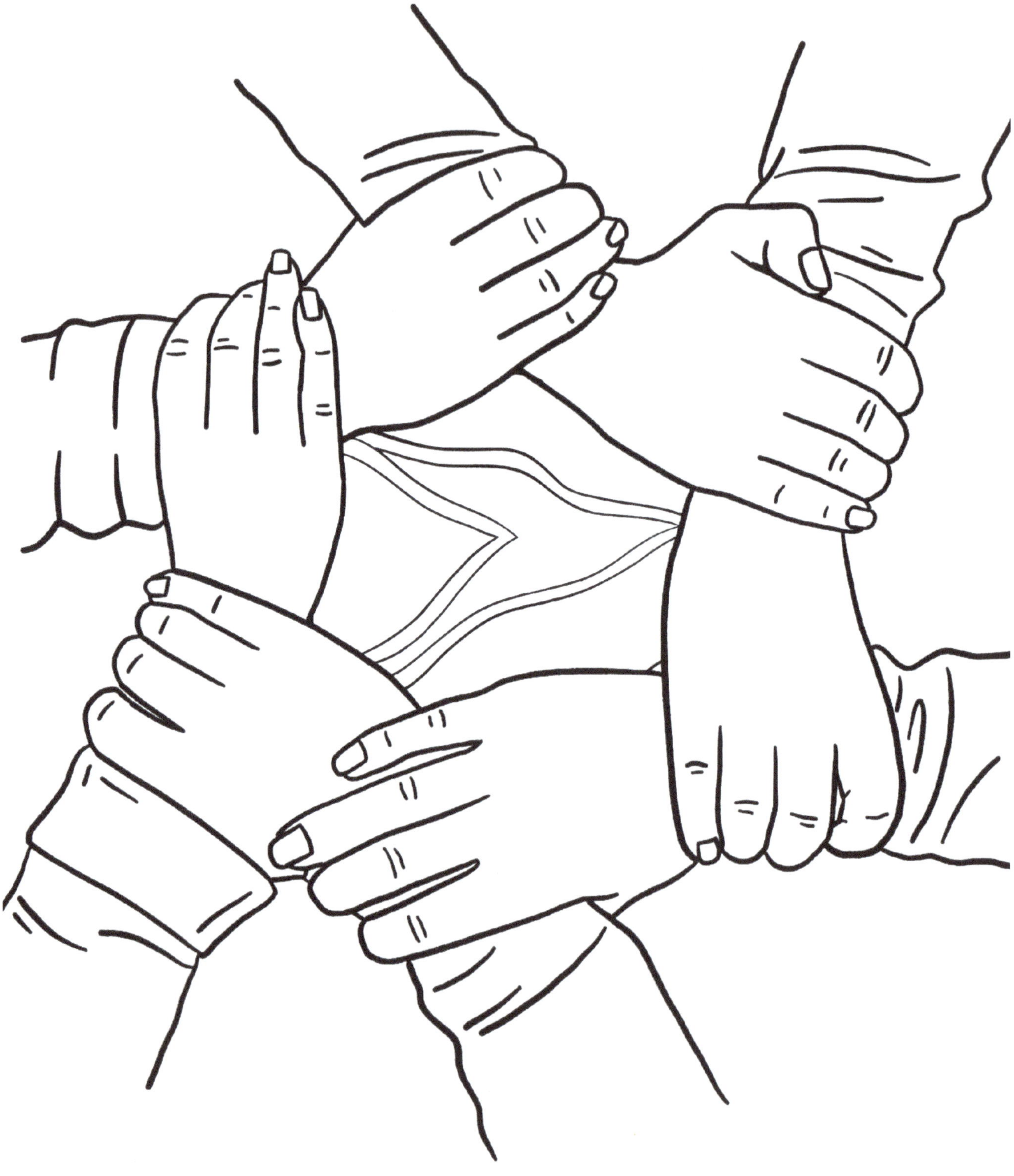

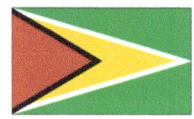

Guyana six ethnic groups
Guyana is home to six ethnic groups – **Amerindian, East Indian, African, Portuguese, European and Chinese**. These groups live in harmony with each other and celebrate each other's culture as if it is their own.

GUYANA COAT OF ARMS

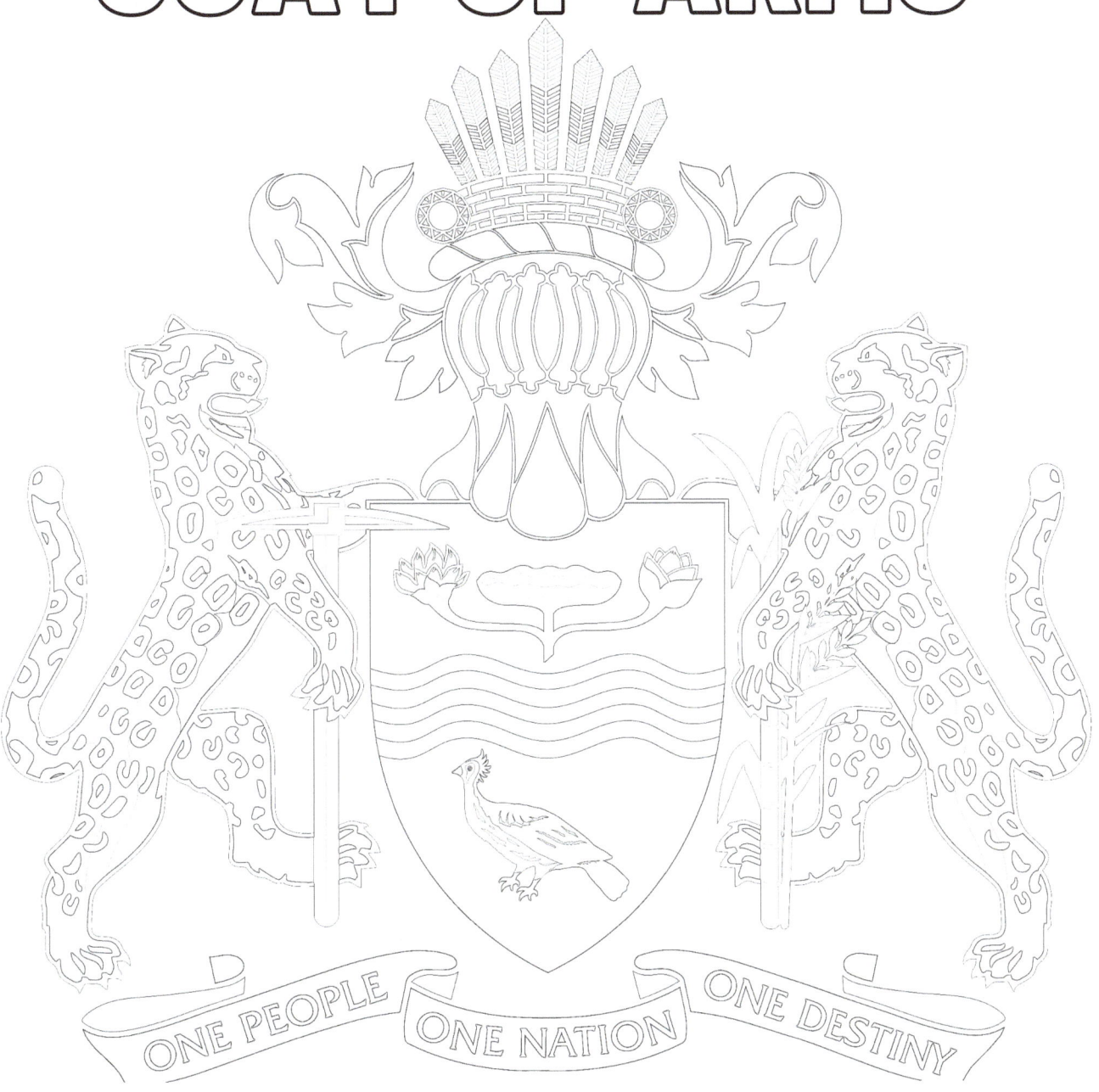

Coat of Arms of Guyana

It includes a crest of an Amerindian head-dress symbolizing the indigenous people of the country, this crest is also called the Cacique's Crown; two diamonds at the sides of the head-dress representing mining industry; a helmet; two jaguars as supporters holding a pick axe, sugar cane, and a stalk of rice (symbolizing Guyana's mining, sugar and rice industries); a shield decorated with the Victoria Amazonica Lily, Guyana's national flower; three blue wavy lines representing the three main rivers of Guyana; and the national bird, the Canje Pheasant (Opisthocomus Hoazin). The national motto, "One people, One Nation, One Destiny", appears on the scroll below the shield.

VICTORIA AMAZONICA

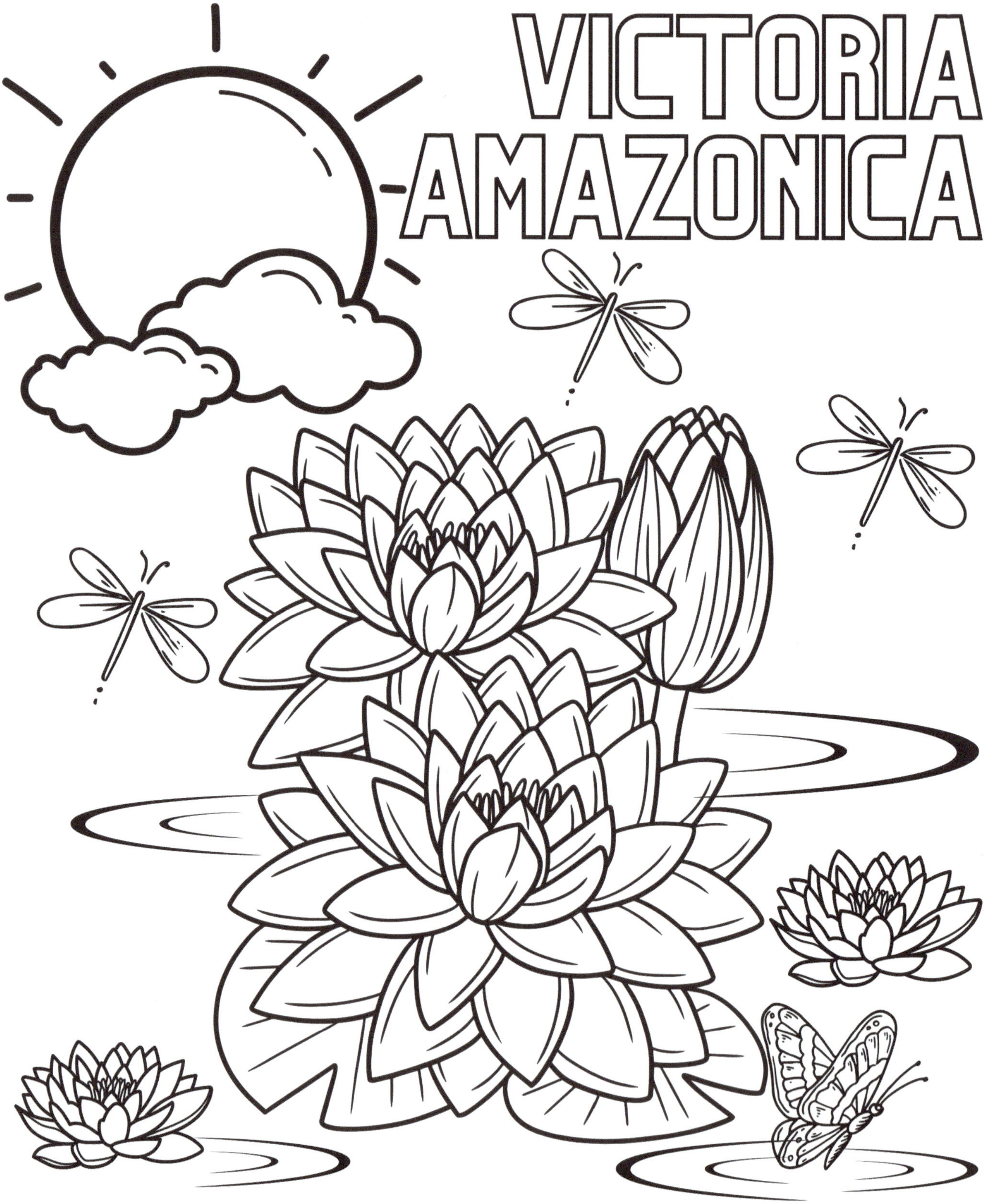

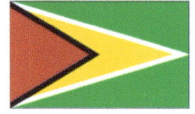 **Guyana National Flower - Victoria Amazonica**
Victoria Amazonica is a species of flowering plant, the second largest of the water lily family Nymphaeaceae. Its native regions are Guyana and tropical South America.

CANJE PHEASANT

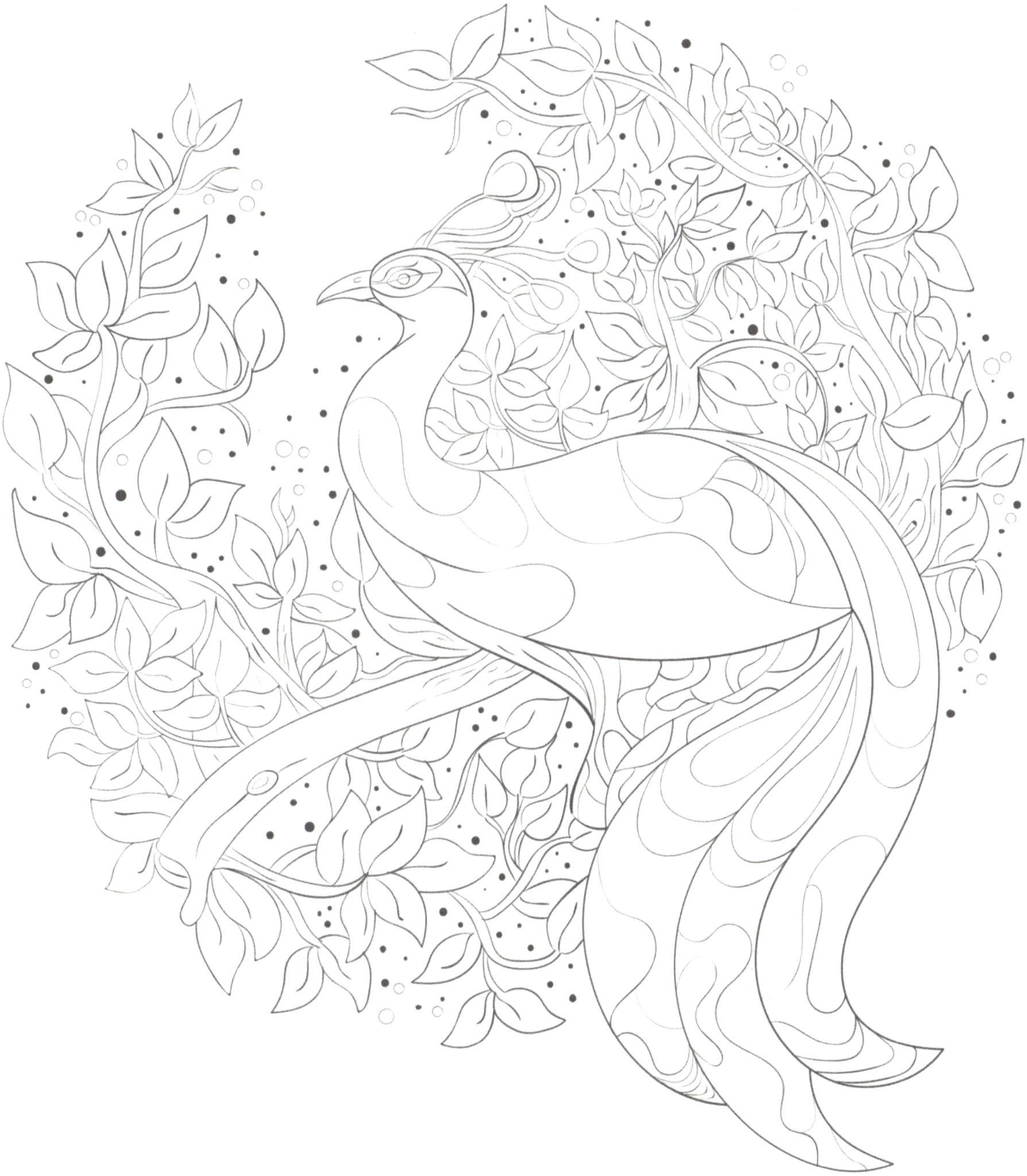

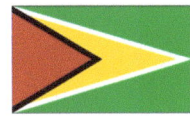

Guyana National Bird- Canje Pheasant or Hoatzin
The Canje Pheasant or Hoatzin is considered a national symbol of Guyana. This bird can be found throughout the year in areas along the banks of the Berbice River and its tributary, the Canje Creek, and to some extent, on the Abary, Mahaicony, and Mahaica Rivers.

PANTHERA ONCA

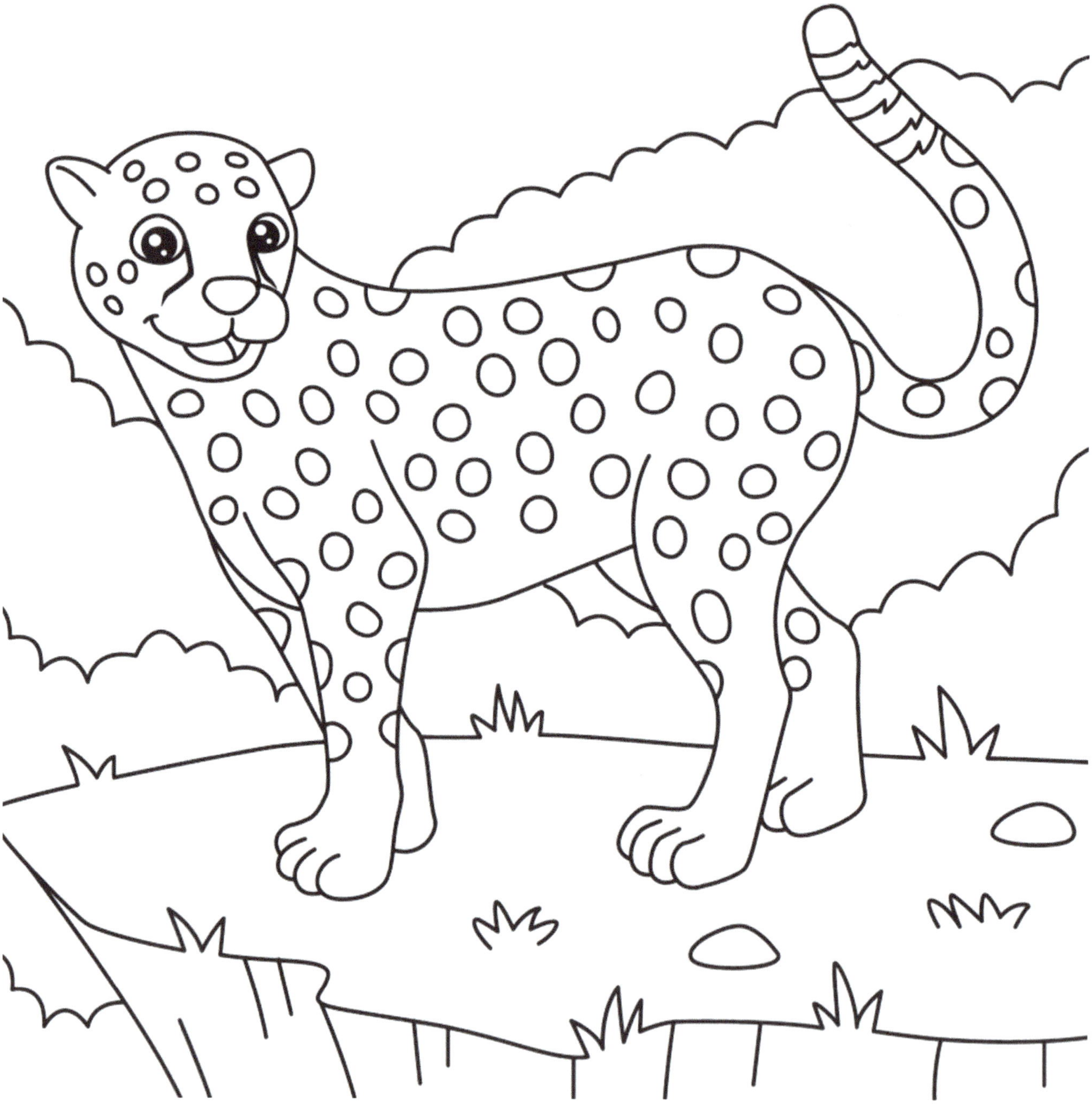

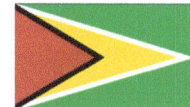

Guyana's National Animal - Jaguar

The Jaguar (Panthera Onca) is considered the largest cat in the Americas and ranges from the southwestern US to Argentina. There is much color variation in jaguars, but in general, they are a tawny golden color on the back and sides with a white underbelly and are spotted with black rosettes all over.

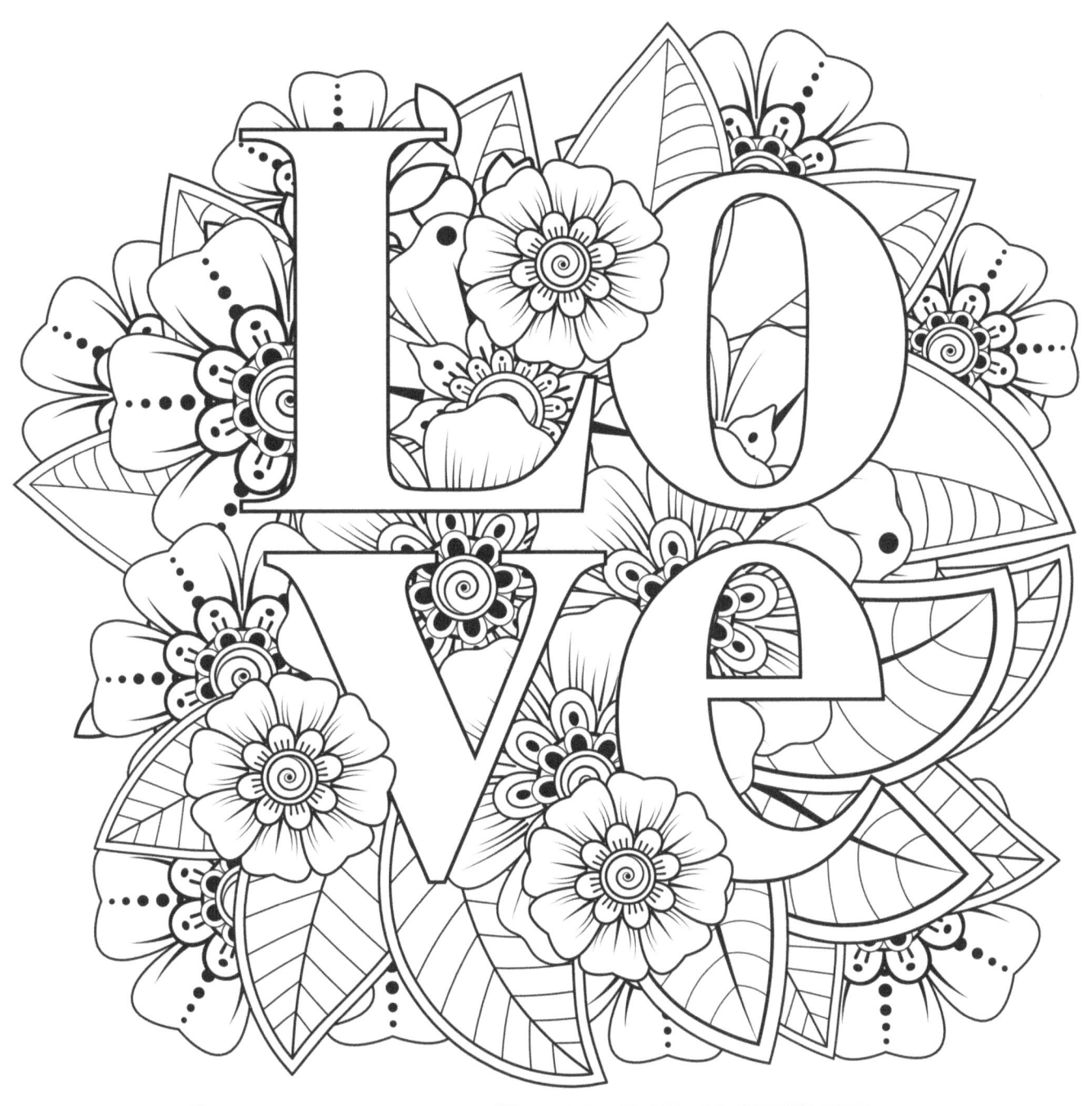

ONE OTHER

ONE PEOPLE | ONE NATION | ONE DESTINY

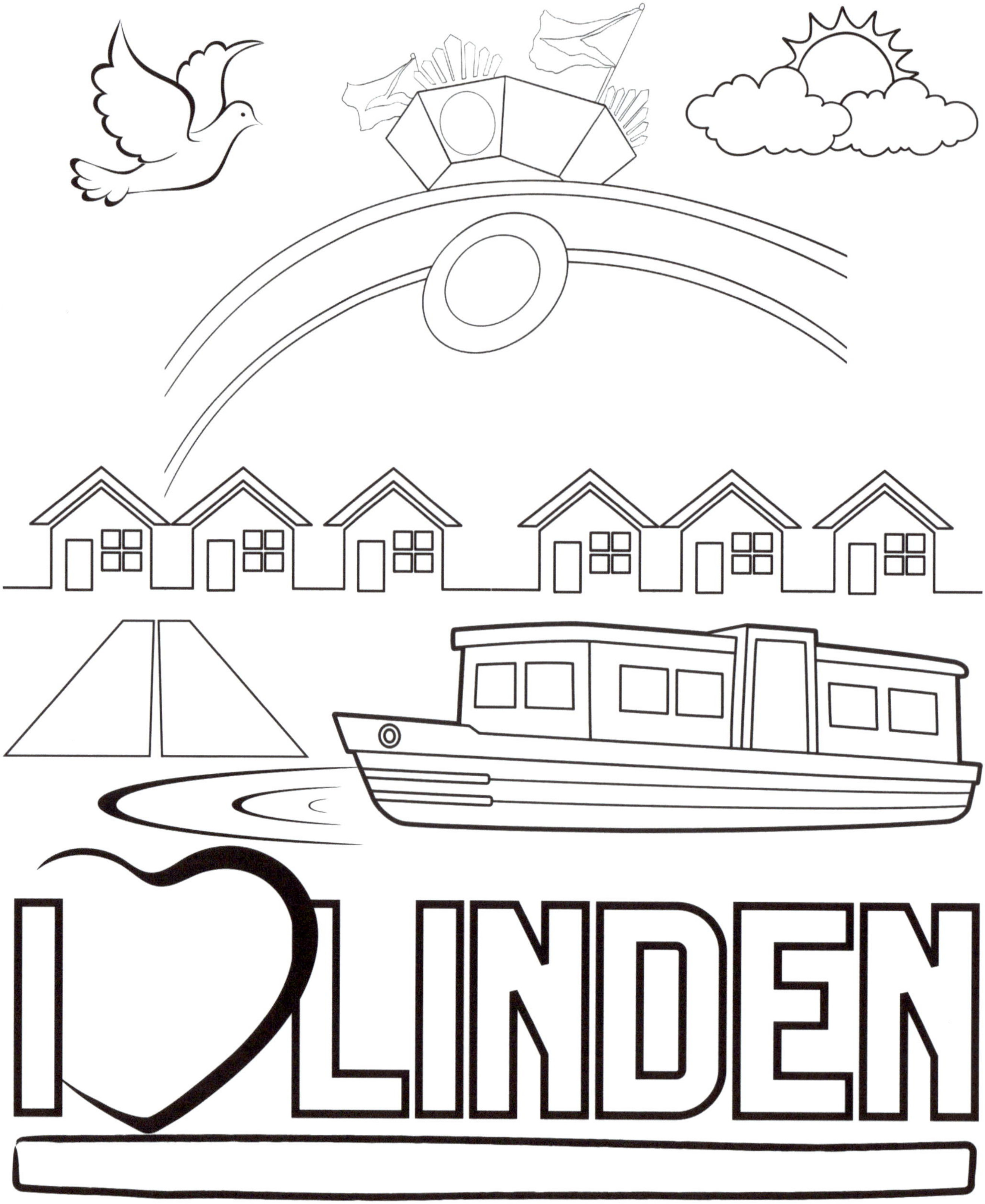

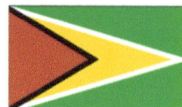
Linden - Region Ten
Linden is the second largest city in Guyana after Georgetown, and capital of the Upper Demerara-Berbice region. It was declared a town in 1970 and includes the communities of MacKenzie, Christianburg, and Wismar. It lies on the Demerara River.

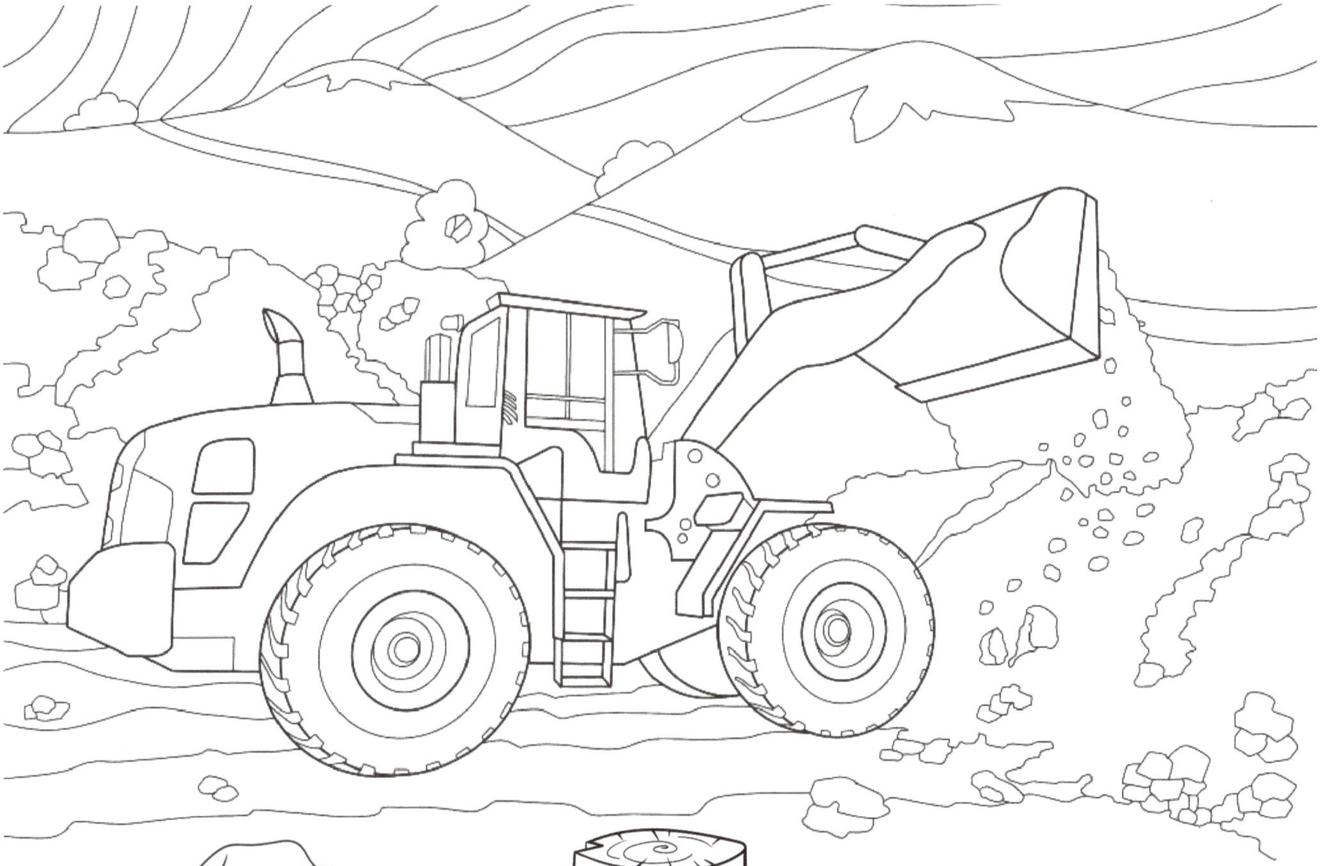

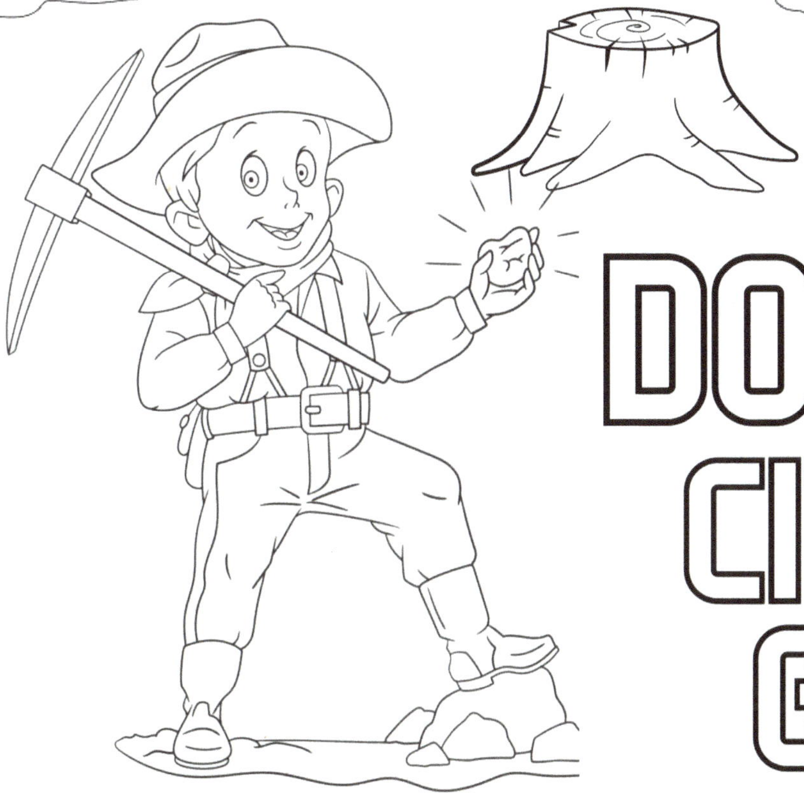

EL DORADO CITY OF GOLD

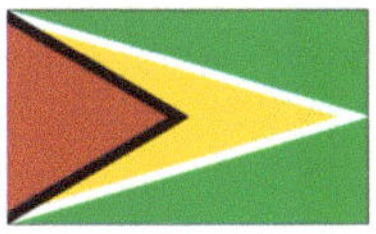

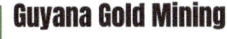

Guyana Gold Mining
Since Guyana gained its independence in 1966, the country's chief economic assets have been its natural resources, mainly its pristine rainforests, sugarcane plantations, rice fields, and bauxite and gold reserves.

CHRISTIANBURG WATER WHEEL

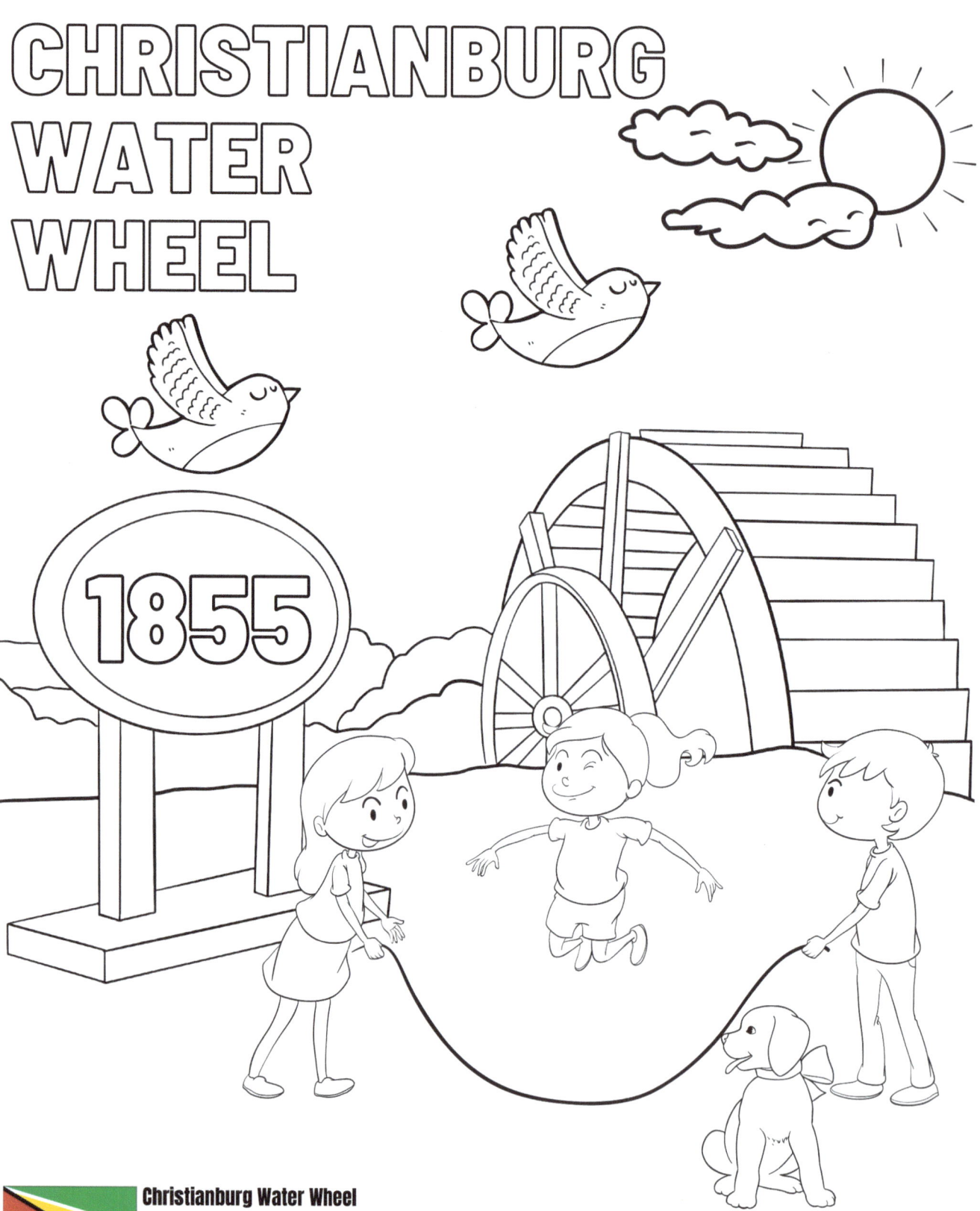

Christianburg Water Wheel
One of the earliest engineering structures to be built in this town was the Christianburg Water Wheel. This hydro-powered sawmill was needed to improve the production of logs and reduce the cost associated with it in which the waterwheel was a part of. This was on a plantation during the latter half of the 1800s. It can therefore be said that the water wheel pioneered the supply of hydroelectricity in the Demerara region.

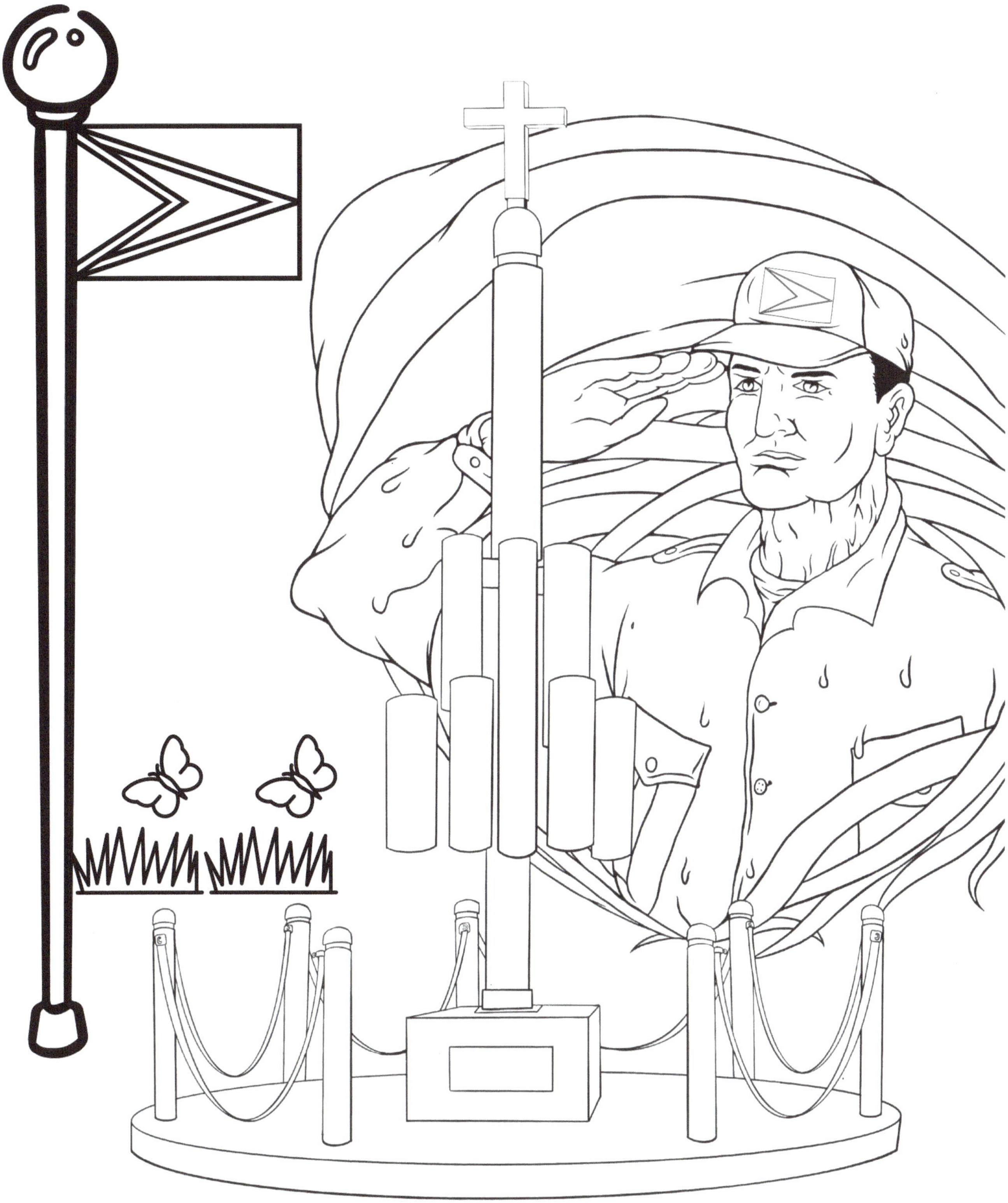

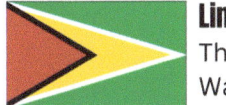
Linden, Guyana Cenotaph
This monument was built to honor the falling Guyanese soldiers of World War I and World War II. The Cenotaph is located on Republic Avenue within the vicinity of the Linden Town Council. Make sure you visit the I LOVE LINDEN monument at The Mayor's Park on Republic Ave

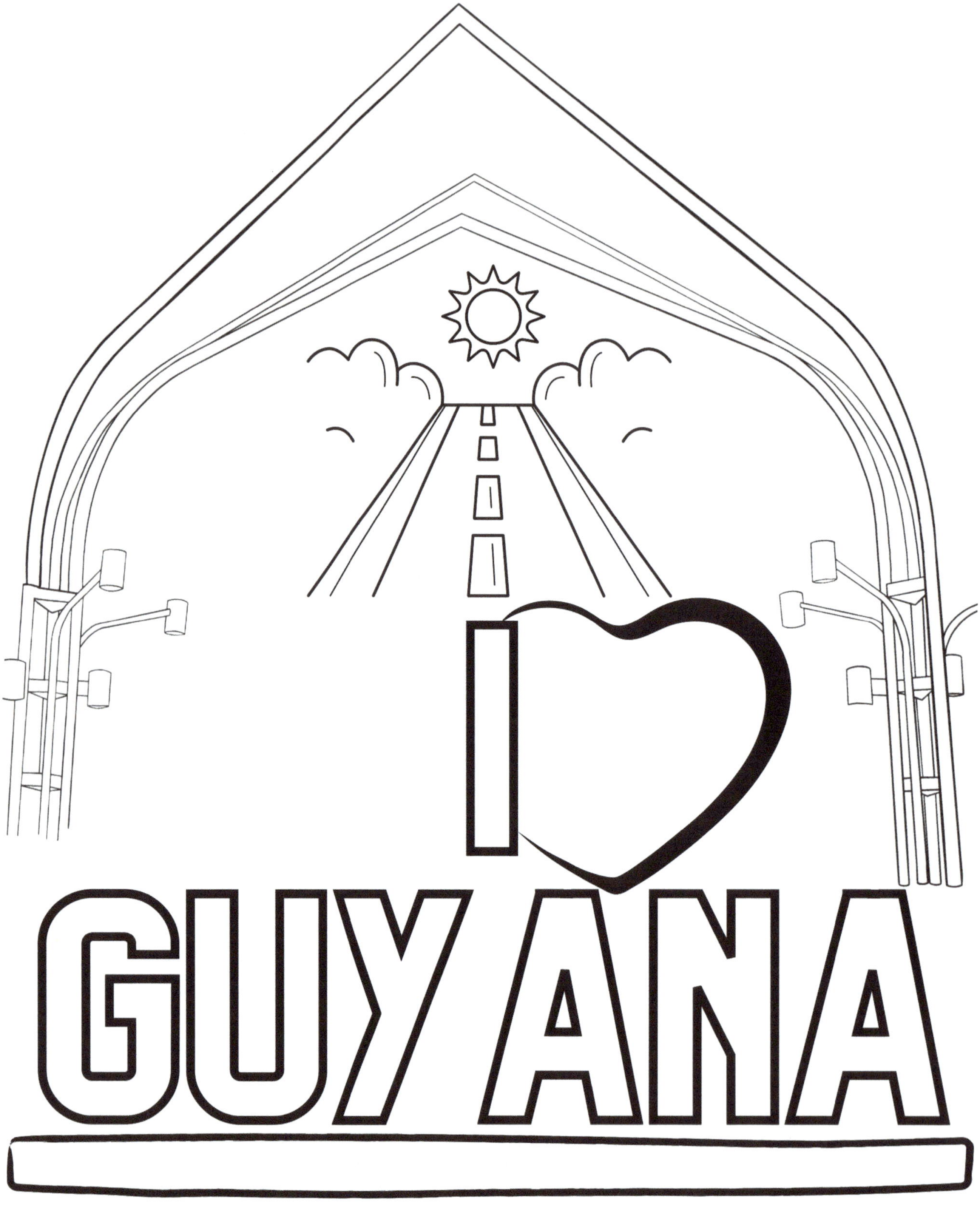

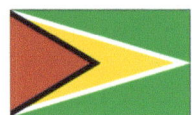

Guyana Independence Arch
The National Independence Arch on Brickdam, near Vlissengen Road, is a gift to the people of Guyana from the Demerara Bauxite Company (DEMBA) commemorating Guyana's Independence from Great Britain on May 26, 1966. Make sure you visit the I Love Guyana monument on Seawall Public Road.

CUFFY SLAVE REBELLION

1763

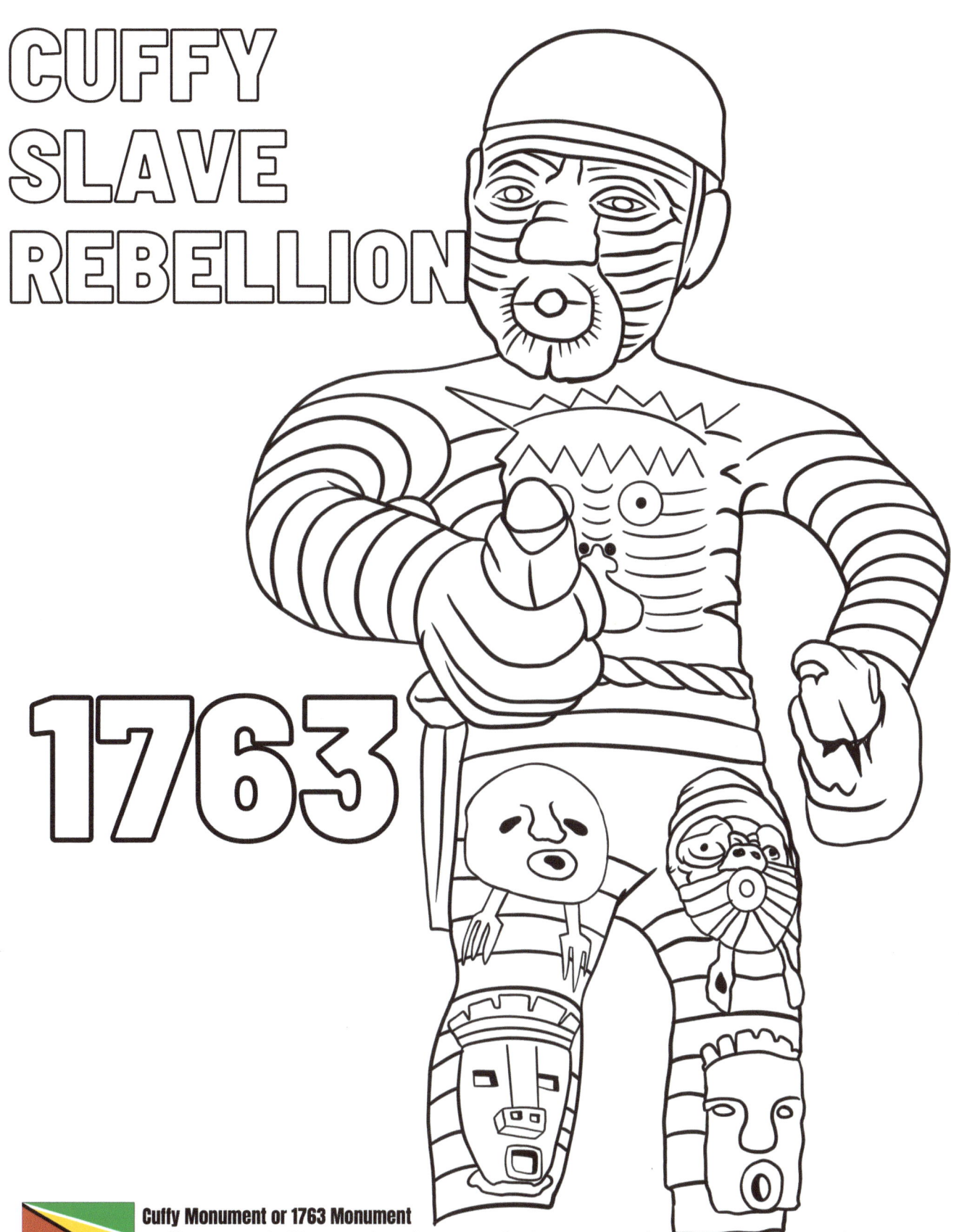

Cuffy Monument or 1763 Monument
Cuffy was a rebellious enslaved person who became a national hero in Guyana. The anniversary of the Cuffy slave rebellion, 23 February, has been Republic Day in Guyana since 1970. Cuffy is commemorated in the 1763 Monument in the Square of the Revolution in the capital Georgetown.

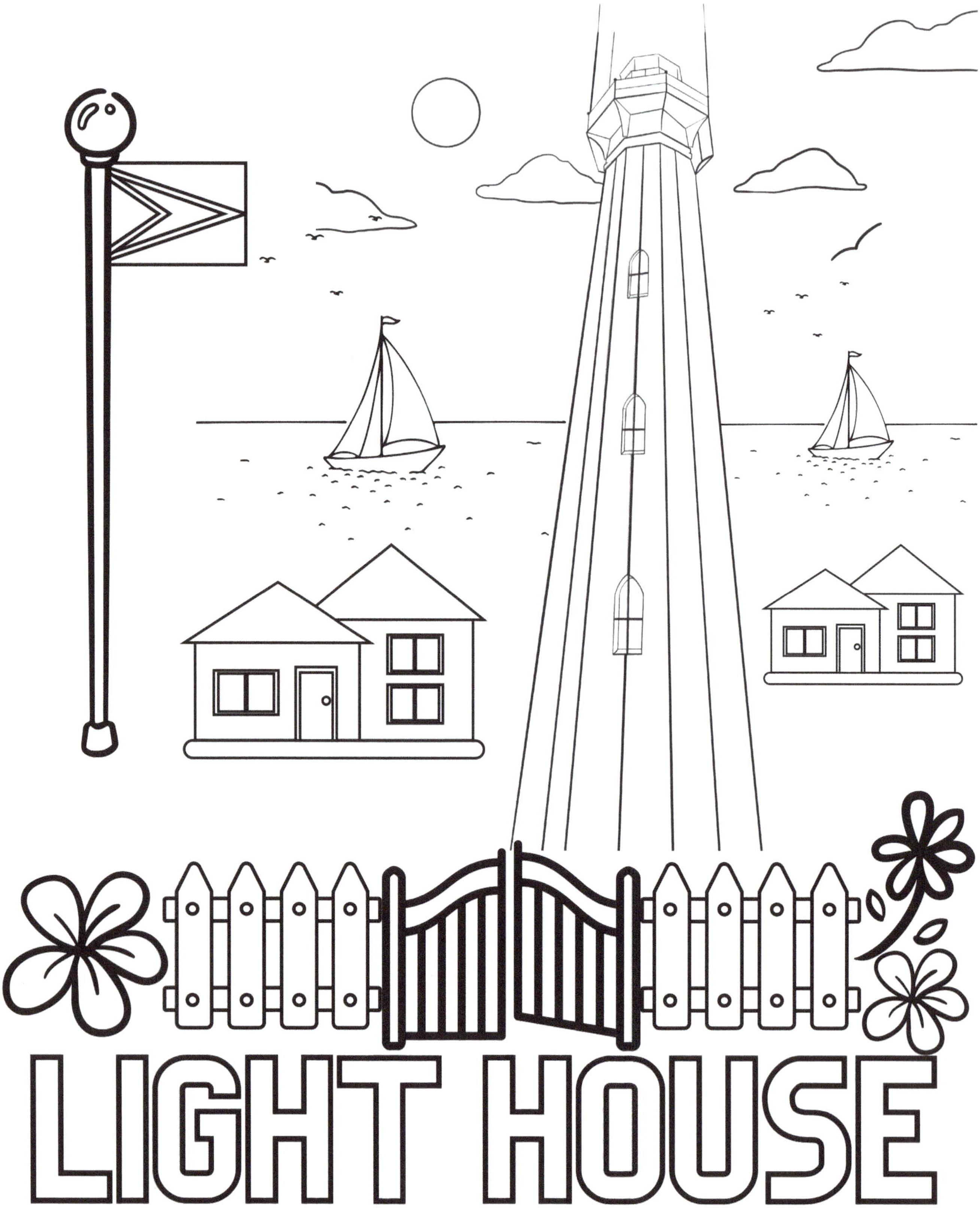

LIGHT HOUSE

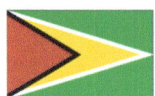

Guyana Light House

The Georgetown Lighthouse was first built by the Dutch in 1817 and then rebuilt in 1830 to help guide ships into the Demerara River from the Atlantic Ocean. The Light House is located at Water Street, Georgetown, Guyana.

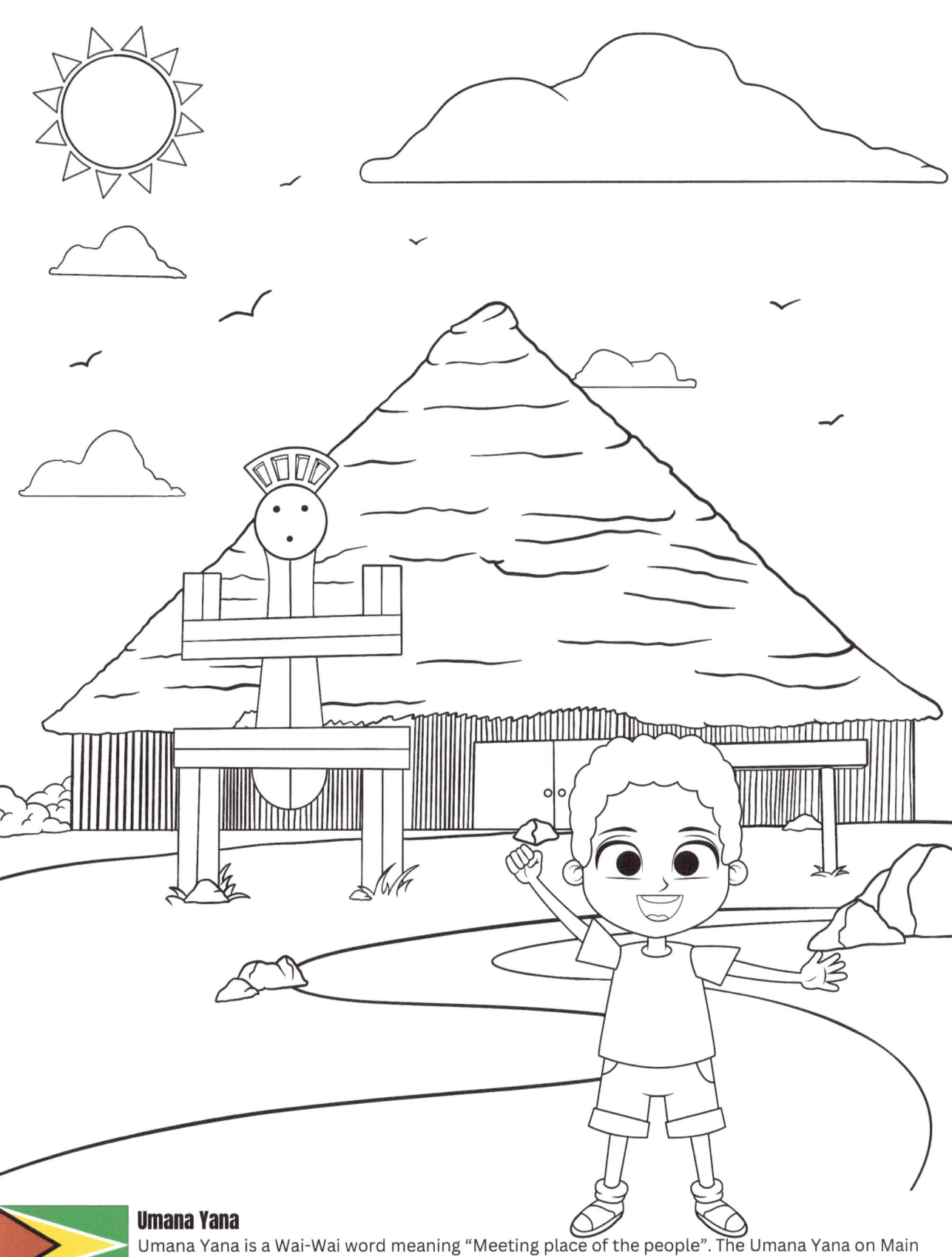

Umana Yana
Umana Yana is a Wai-Wai word meaning "Meeting place of the people". The Umana Yana on Main Street, next to the Pegasus Hotel, is a conical palm thatched hut (benab) erected for the Non-Aligned Foreign Ministers Conference in Guyana in August 1972 as a V.I.P. Lounge and recreation centre. It is now a permanent structure and admired part of Georgetown's scenery, and used as an exhibition and conference centre.

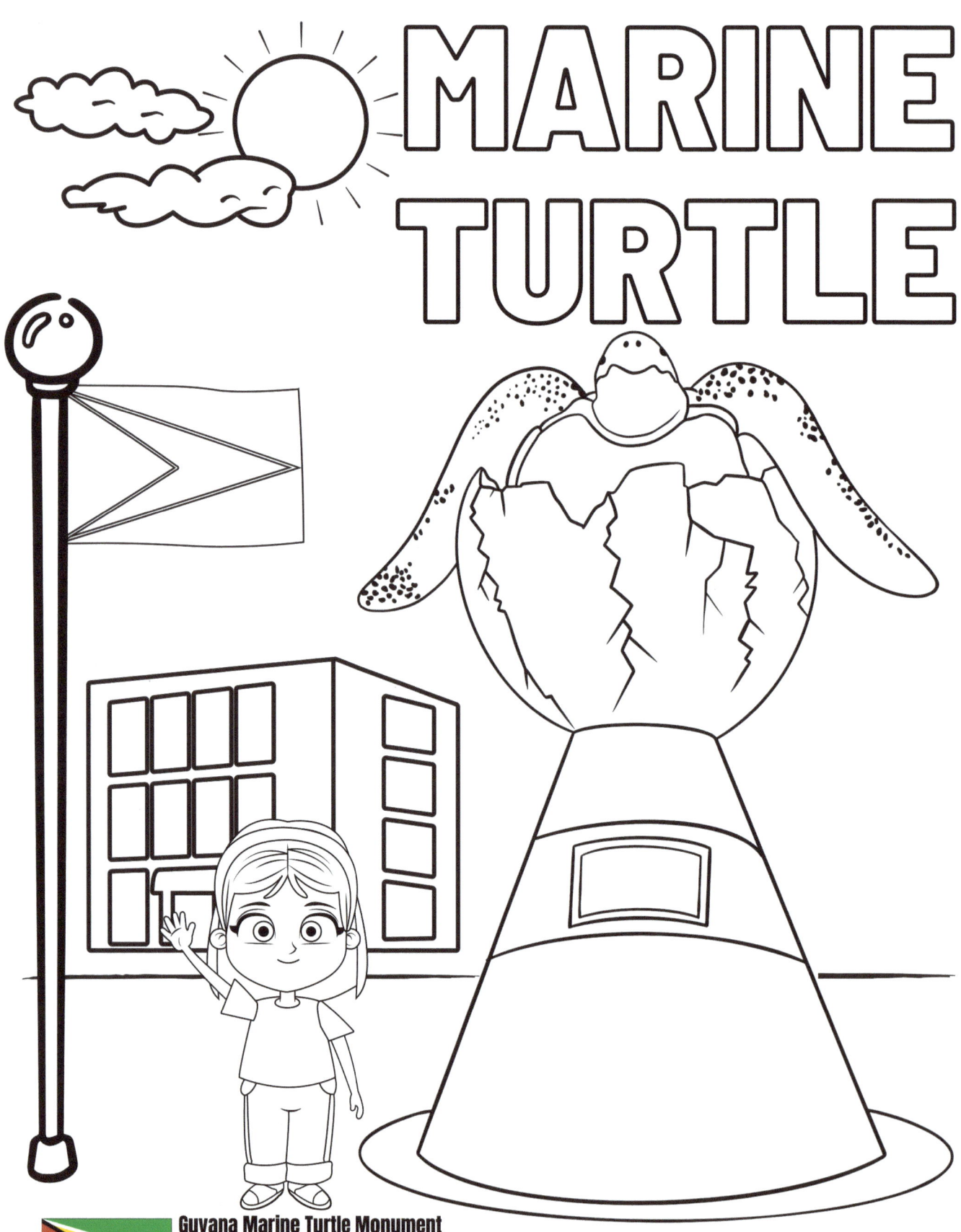

Guyana Marine Turtle Monument
The monument was unveiled in 2001, by the Guyana Marine Turtle Conservation Society to raise awareness towards our natural heritage. The monument is located on SeaWall Public Rd, Georgetown next to the **Umana Yana** and the **I LOVE GUYANA** Sign.

SEAWALL BANDSTAND

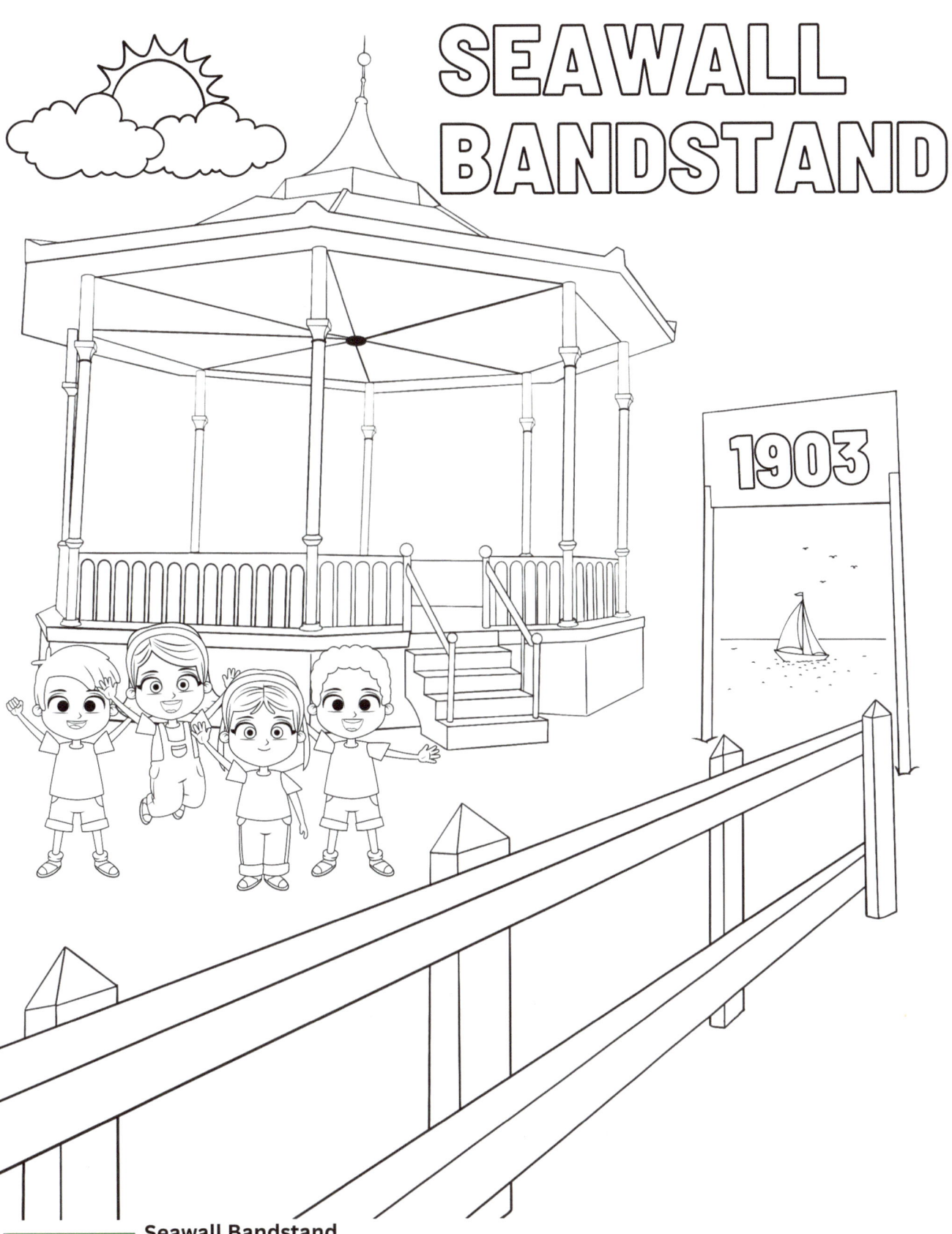

Seawall Bandstand
The Georgetown Seawall Bandstand is an iron bandstand that is situated on the western end of Georgetown Seawall in Guyana. It is one of three bandstands in Georgetown, the other two being situated in the Botanical Gardens and the Promenade Gardens. The Georgetown Seawall Bandstand was built in 1903 with public funds as a memorial to Queen Victoria.

STABROEK MARKET

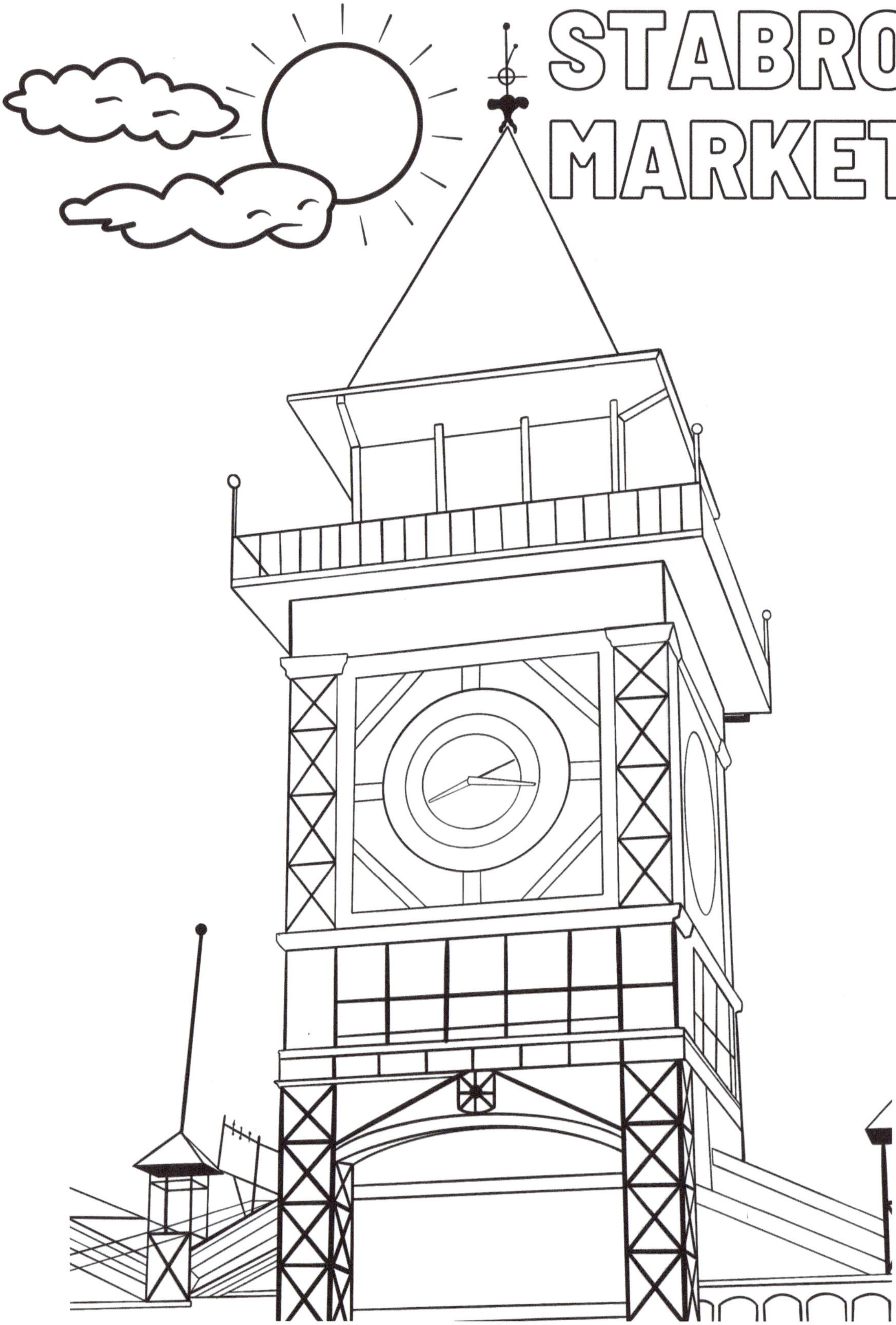

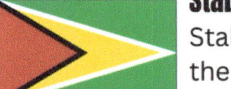

Stabroek Market
Stabroek Market is the largest market of Georgetown, Guyana. Located in the centre of the capital city, the market is housed in an iron and steel structure with a prominent clock tower.

CUMMINGS LODGE ARCH

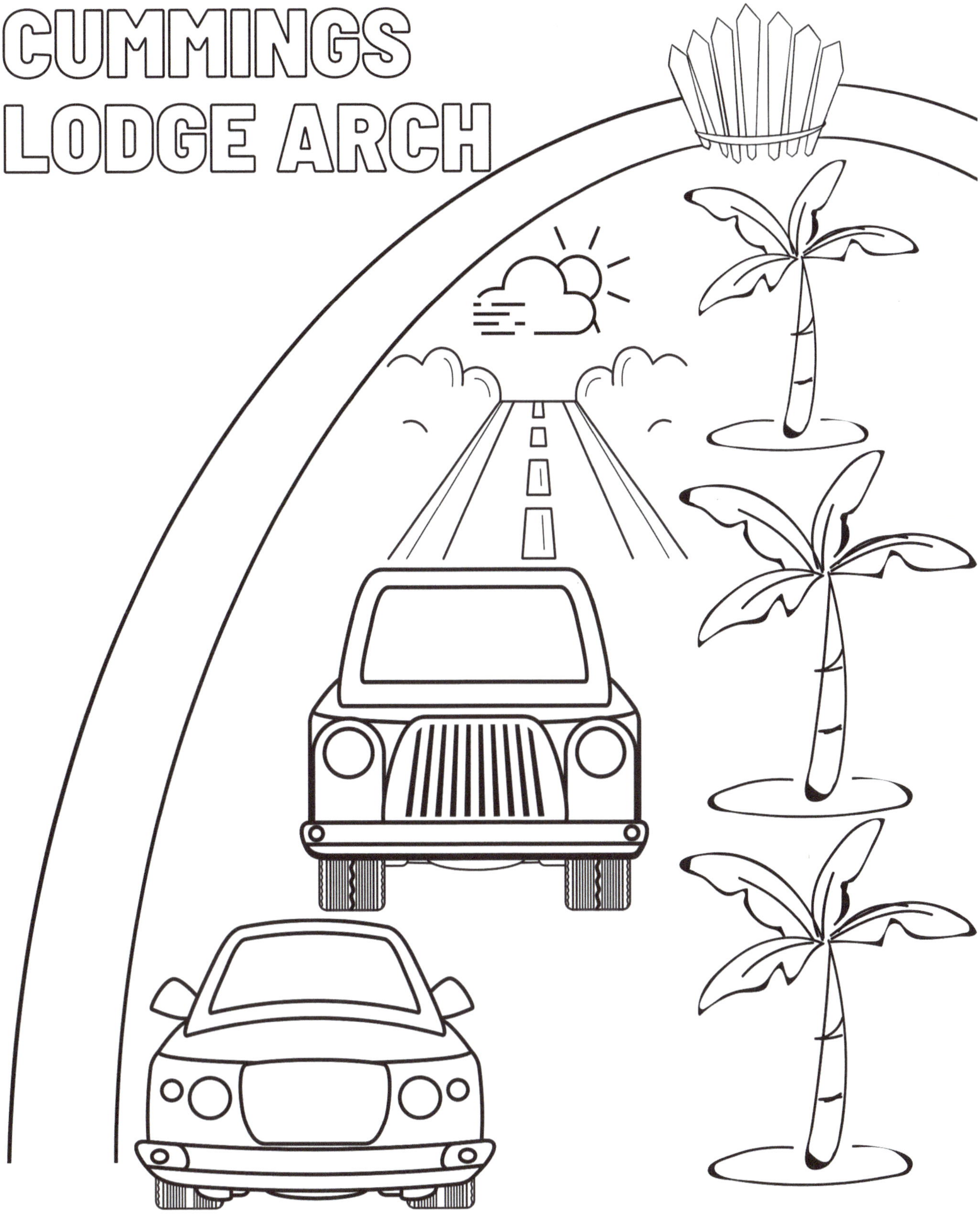

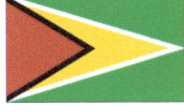

Guyana Cummings Lodge Arch
Cummings Lodge, a suburb of Georgetown, is located 8 kilometers (4.97 miles) east of the capital city. The arch which was installed on the Rupert Craig Highway serves as a visual indicator of the boundaries of Georgetown (Cummings Lodge) and the East Coast (Industry).

ST. GEORGE'S CATHEDRAL

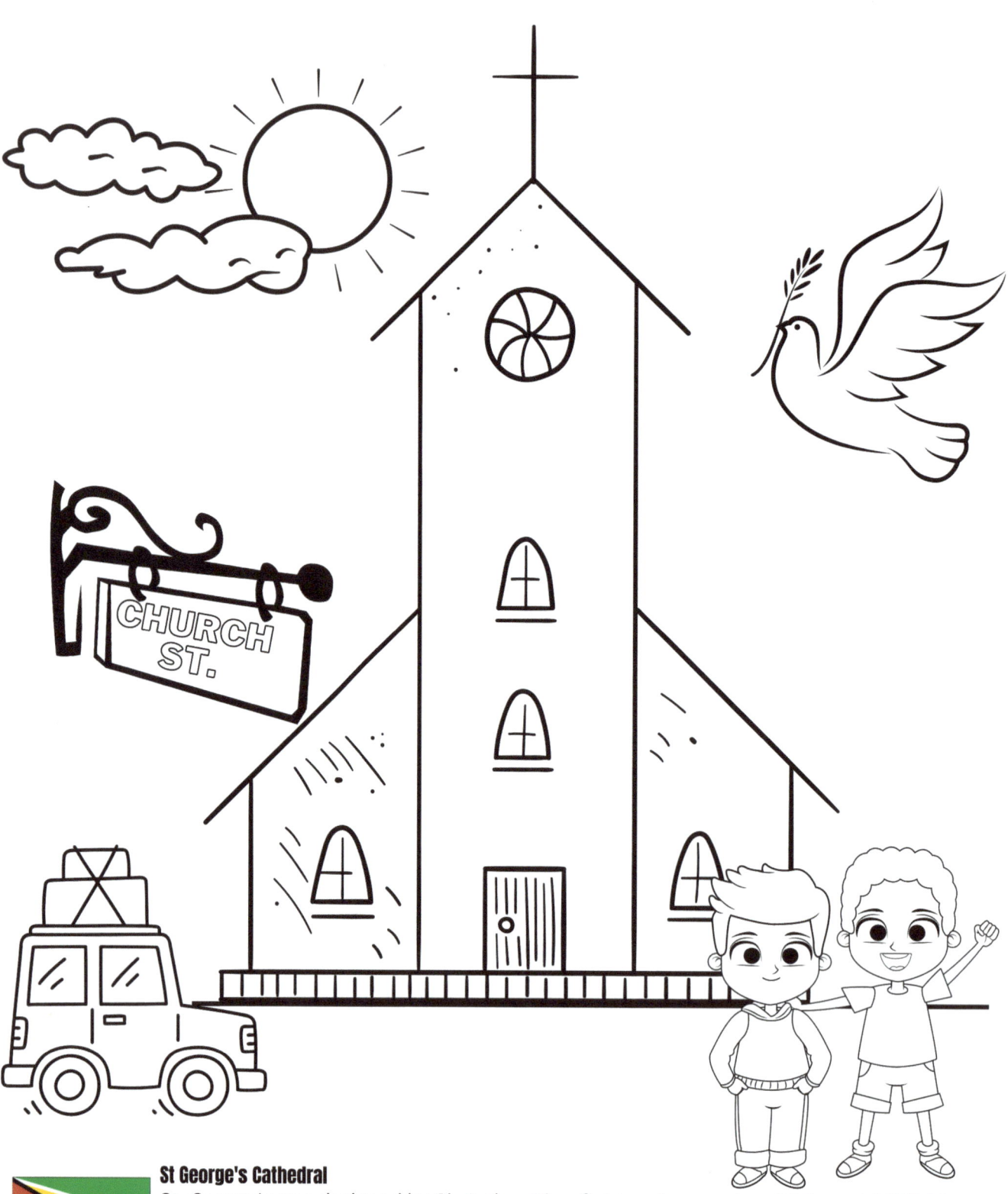

St George's Cathedral
St. George's was designed by Sir Arthur Blomfield and opened on 24 August 1892. The building was completed in 1899. It is located on Church Street in Georgetown and has been designated a national monument.

MASHRAMANI

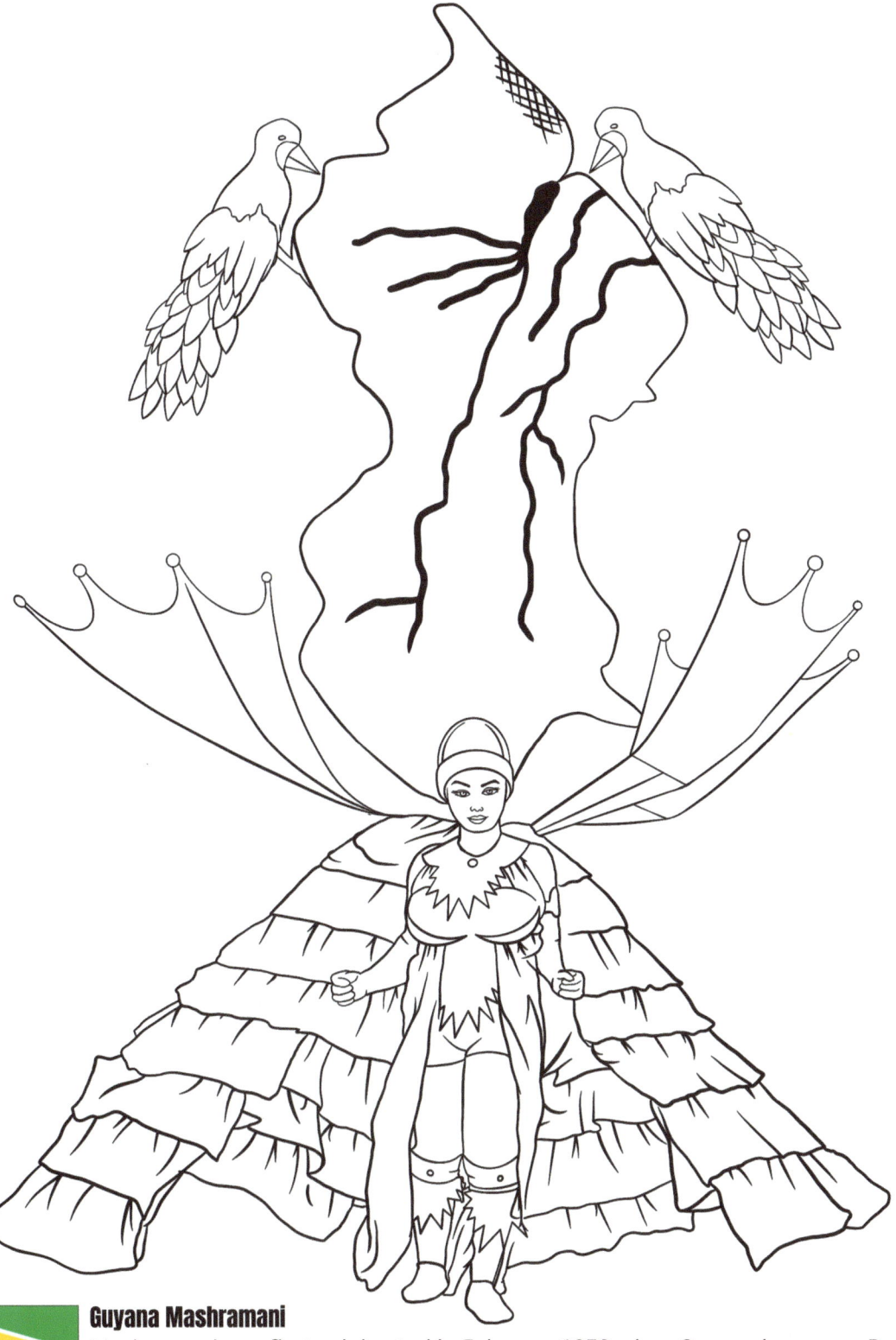

Guyana Mashramani
Mashramani was first celebrated in February 1970 when Guyana became a Republic. Recognizing that there was a need for a cultural festival steeped in local tradition, the Jaycees of Linden who had been organizing Independence Carnival in Mackenzie since 1966, began searching for a name to replace Carnival.

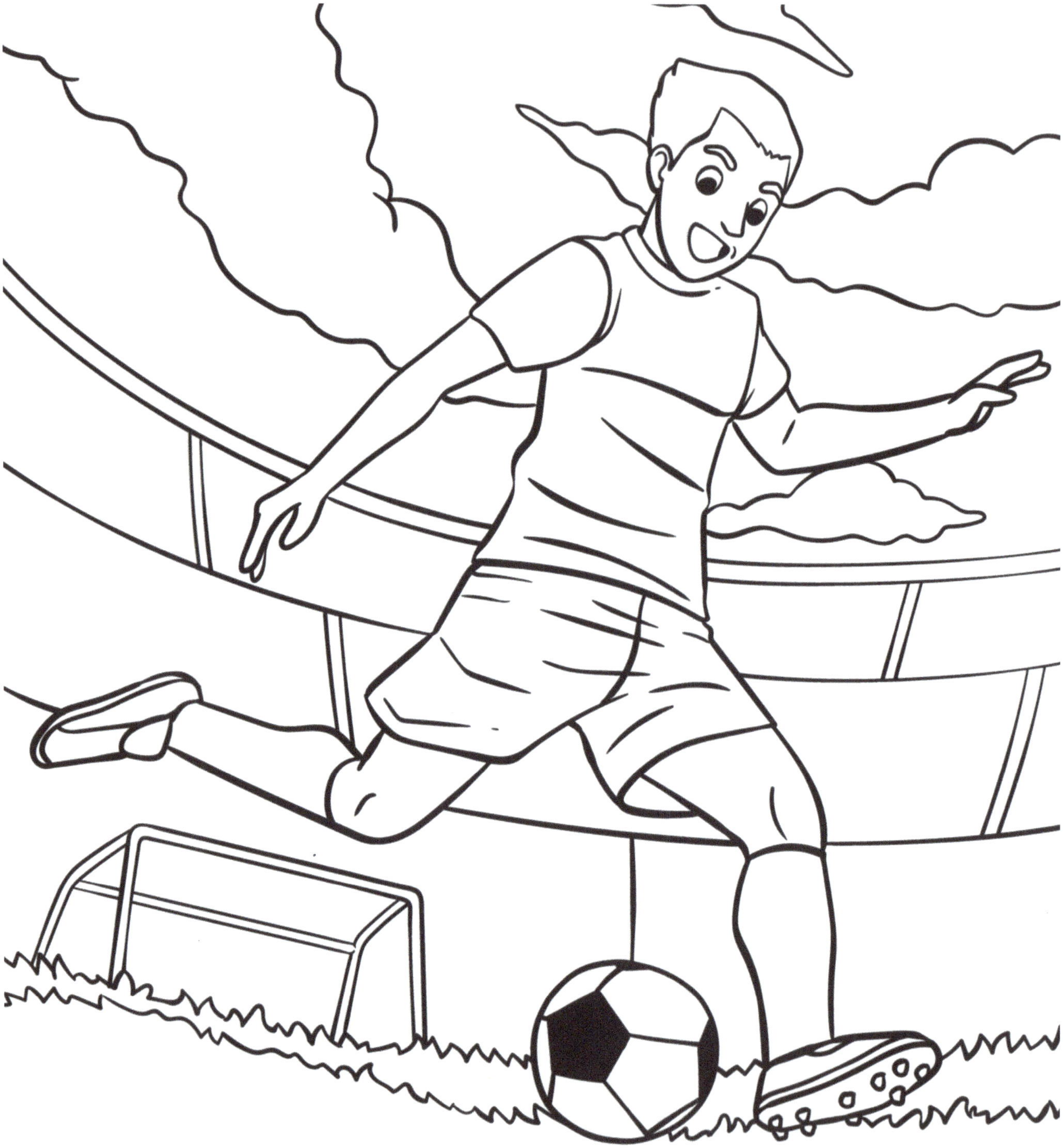

GUYANA GOLDEN JAGUARS

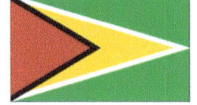

Guyana Golden Jaguars
The Guyana national football team, nicknamed the Golden Jaguars, represents Guyana in international football and is controlled by the Guyana Football Federation. It is one of three South American nations to be a member of the Caribbean Football Union of CONCACAF alongside Suriname and French Guiana.

AMAZON WARRIORS CPL

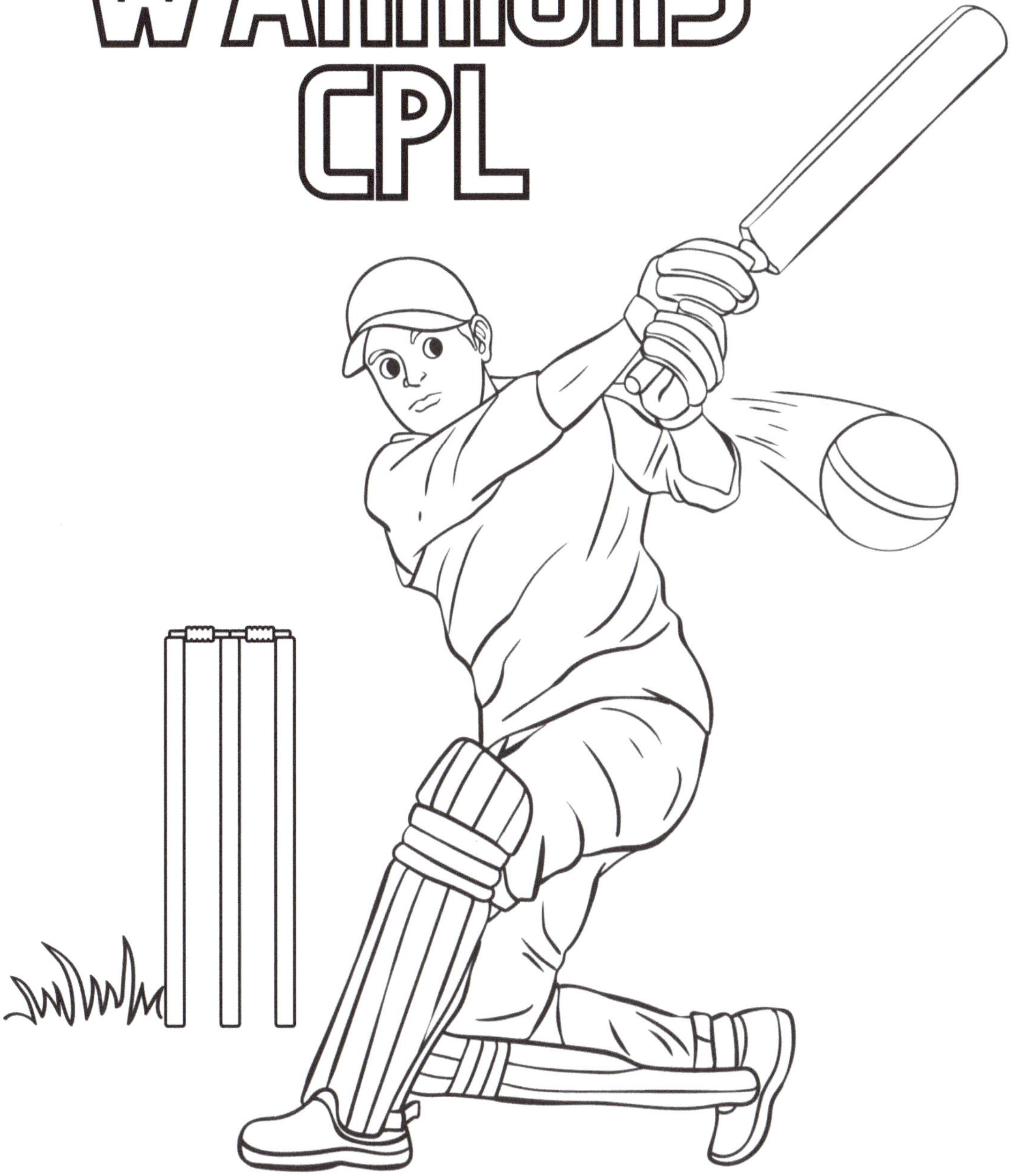

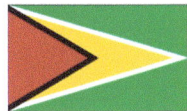

Guyana Amazon warriors
The Guyana Amazon Warriors is a franchise cricket team of the Caribbean Premier League based in Providence, Georgetown, Guyana. The team is the representative cricket team of Guyana in the Caribbean Premier League. It was one of the six teams created in 2013 for the inaugural season of the tournament.

KITE DAY

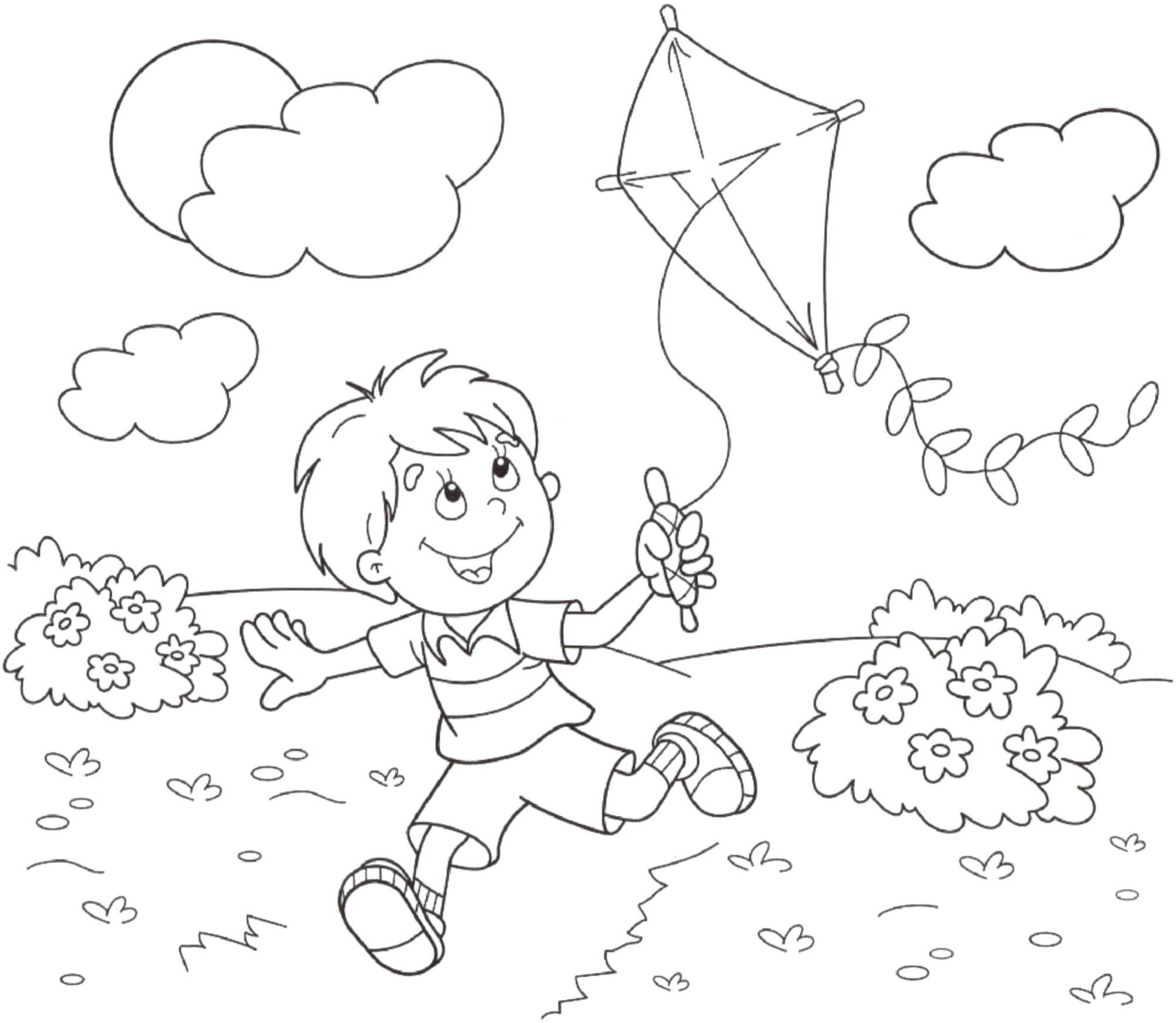

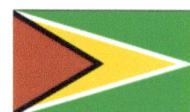

Guyana National Kite Day
Kite flying is an annual tradition in the country of Guyana, South America. Kite flying activities are held every year during the Easter Holidays.

WAKANDA FOREVER

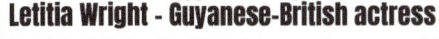

Letitia Wright - Guyanese-British actress

Letitia Michelle Wright was born on 31 October 1993 in Georgetown, Guyana. Her family moved to London, England, when she was seven years old and she attended Northumberland Park Community School. Letitia Wright is known for movies like: Black Panther, Infinity War, and Wakanda Forever. These are just a few of the movies she has stared in. We are proud to see one of our own "Guyanese" represent Guyana so gracefully.

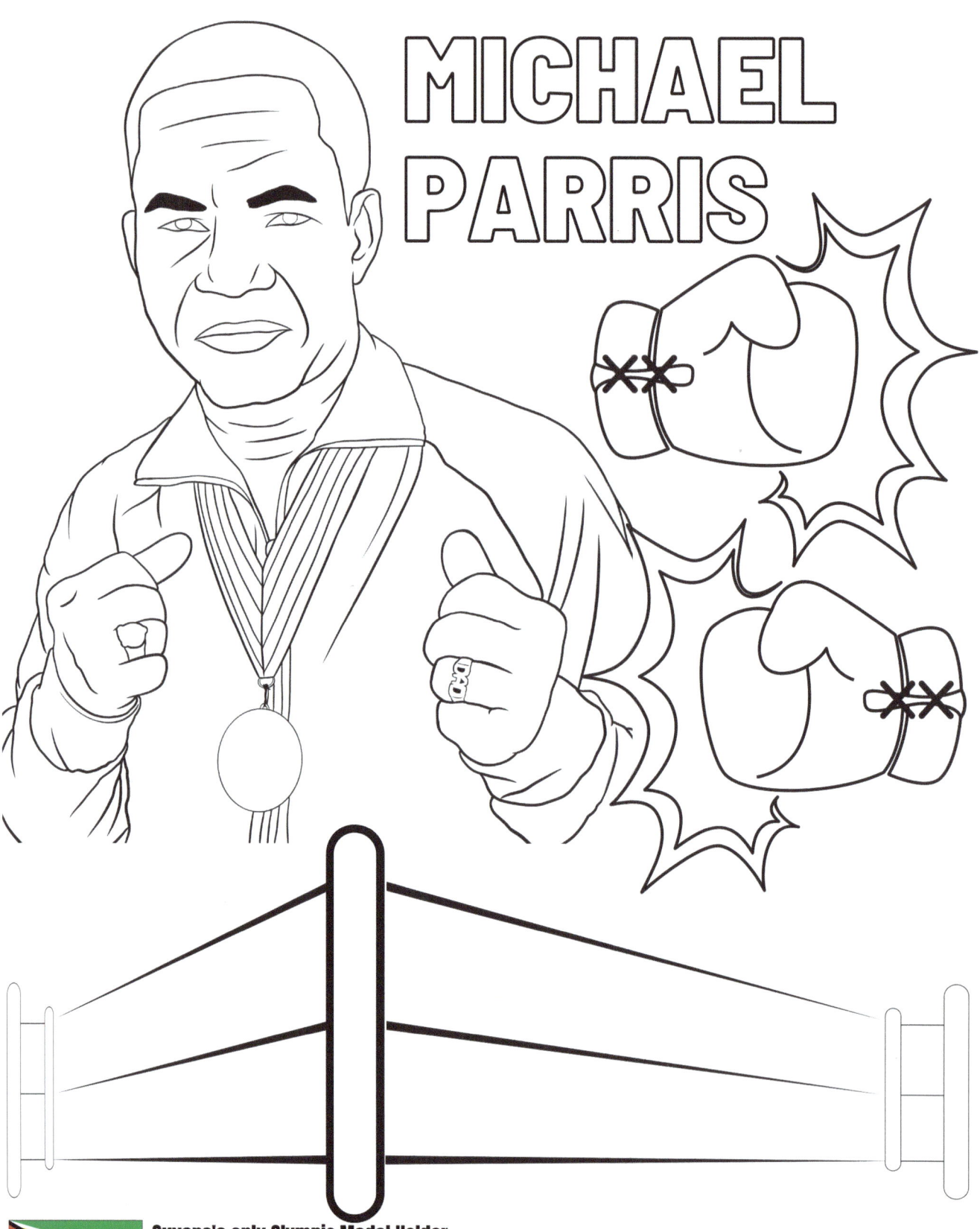

Guyana's only Olympic Medal Holder
Michael Parris (born October 4, 1957), aka Michael Anthony, is a retired boxer from Guyana, who competed in the bantamweight division at the 1980 Summer Olympics in Moscow, Soviet Union. There he won the **bronze** medal (Guyana's only ever medal at the Olympics).

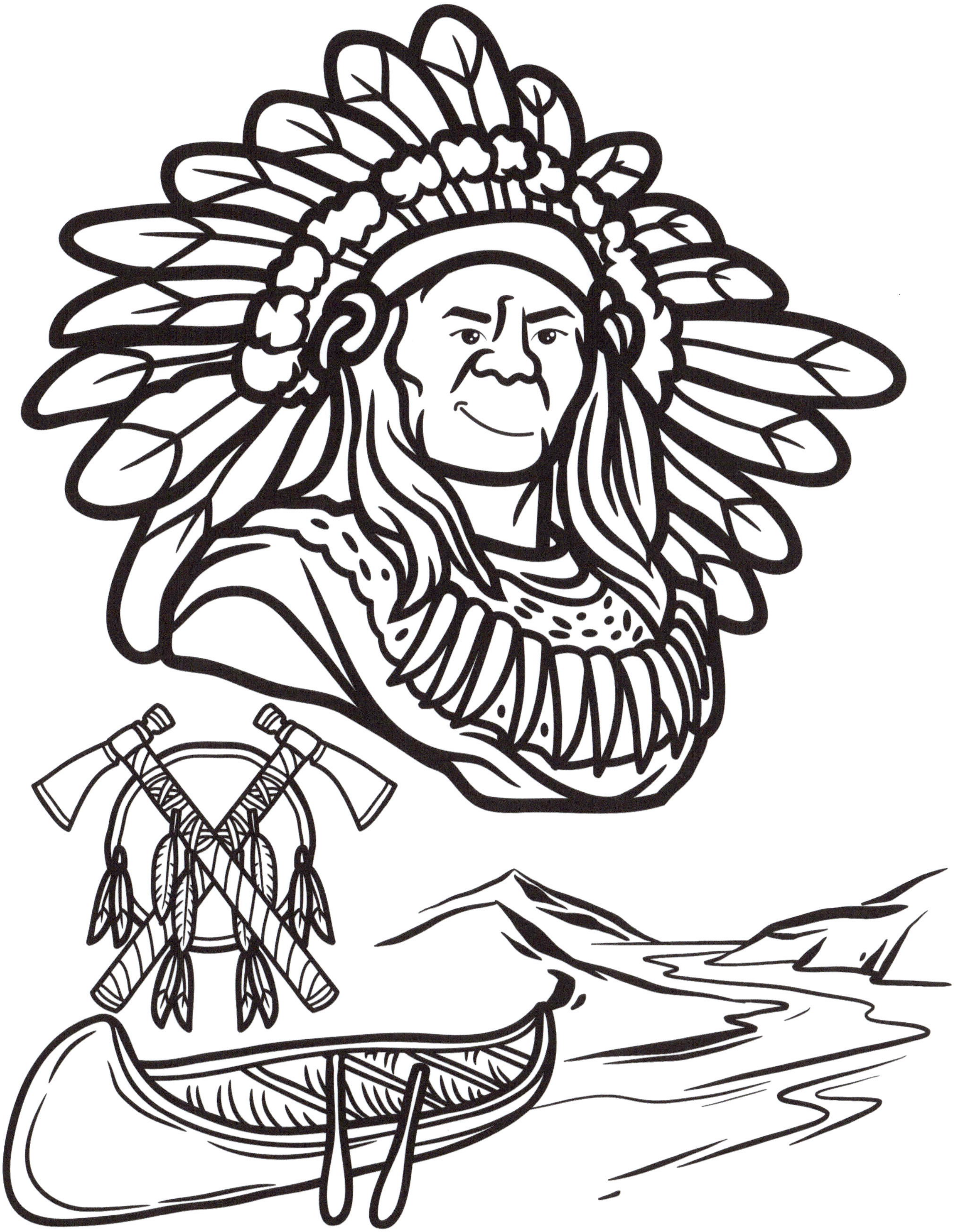

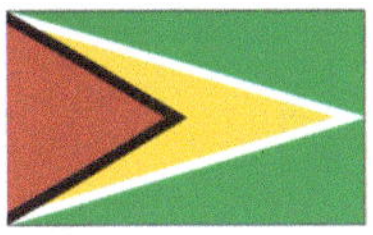

Amerindian tribes in Guyana

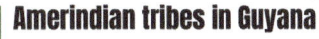

In Guyana, the interior Amerindians are classified into six groups: Akawaio (Kapohn), Arekuna, Patamona, Waiwai, Macusi, and Wapishana. All of the interior Amerindians originally spoke Carib languages, with the exception of the Wapishana, whose language is of the Arawak-Taino family.

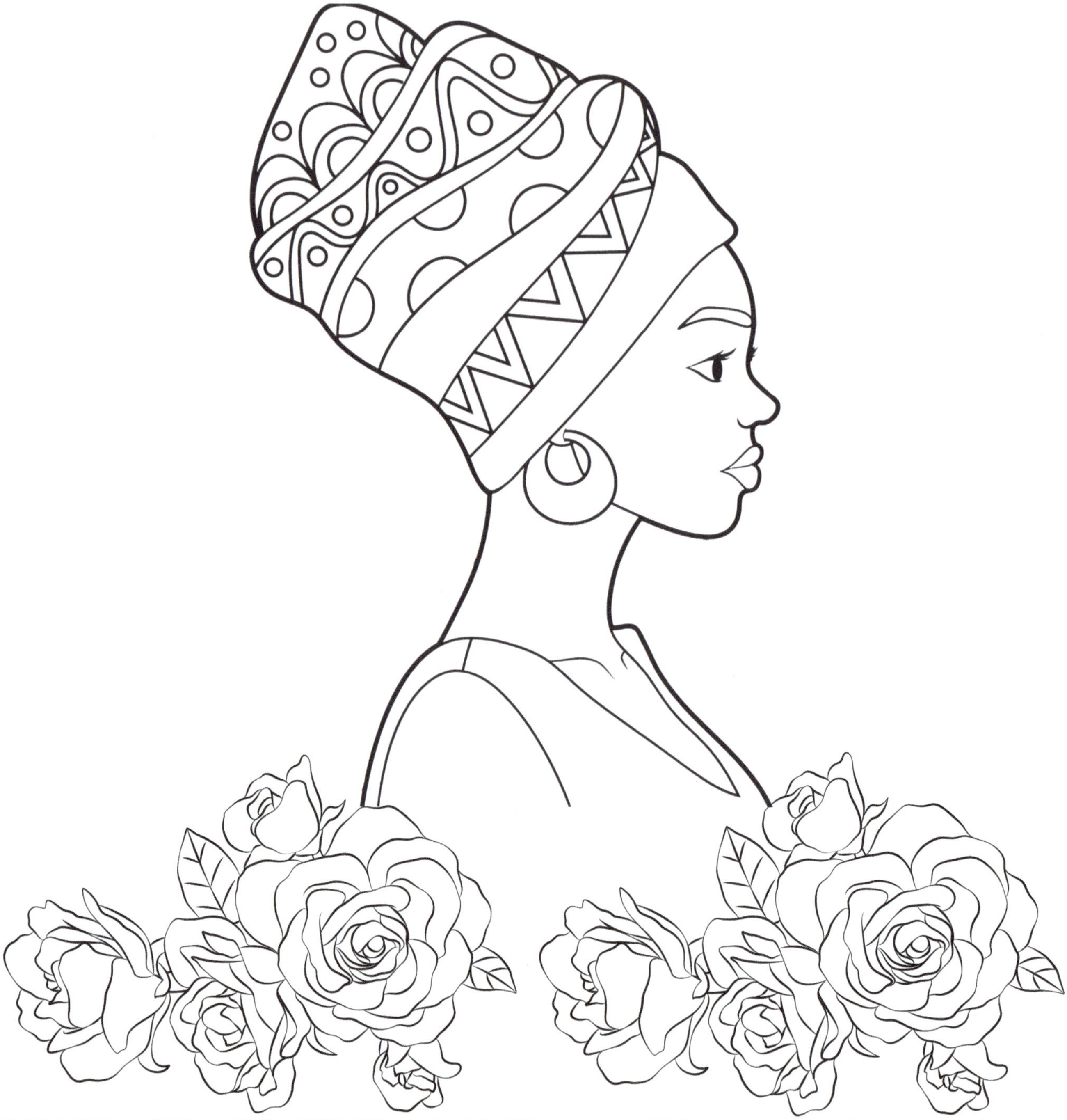

EMANCIPATION

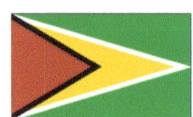

Guyana Emancipation Day

Emancipation Day in Guyana is annually observed on August 1st. It marks the abolition of slavery in Guyana and commemorates the end of years of dehumanization and the resurgence of the African spirit. The holiday is significant not just as a calendar event but as a new lease of life for the Guyanese nation as we know it.

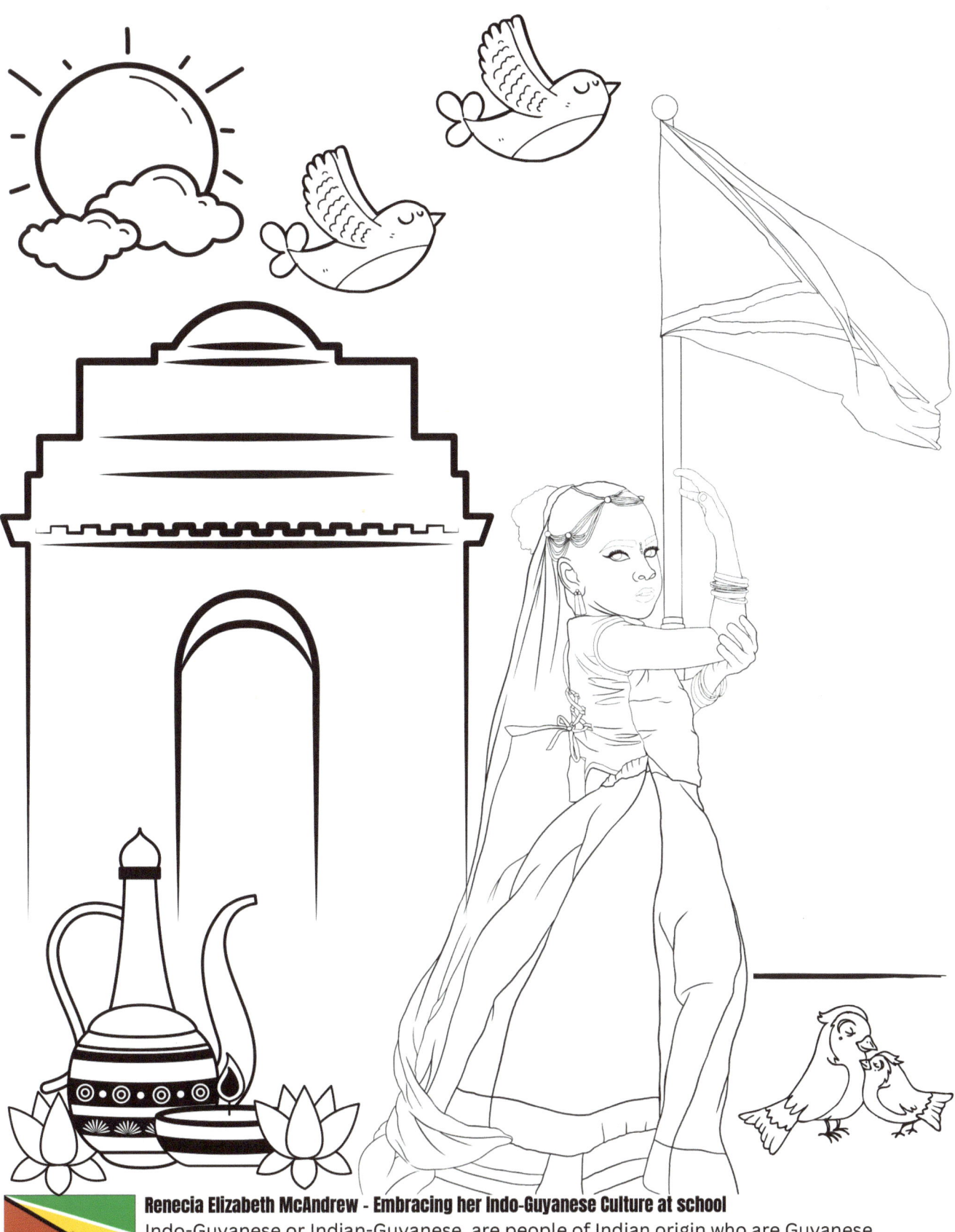

Renecia Elizabeth McAndrew - Embracing her Indo-Guyanese Culture at school
Indo-Guyanese or Indian-Guyanese, are people of Indian origin who are Guyanese nationals tracing their ancestry to the Indian subcontinent. They are the descendants of indentured servants and settlers who migrated from India beginning in 1838 during the time of the British.

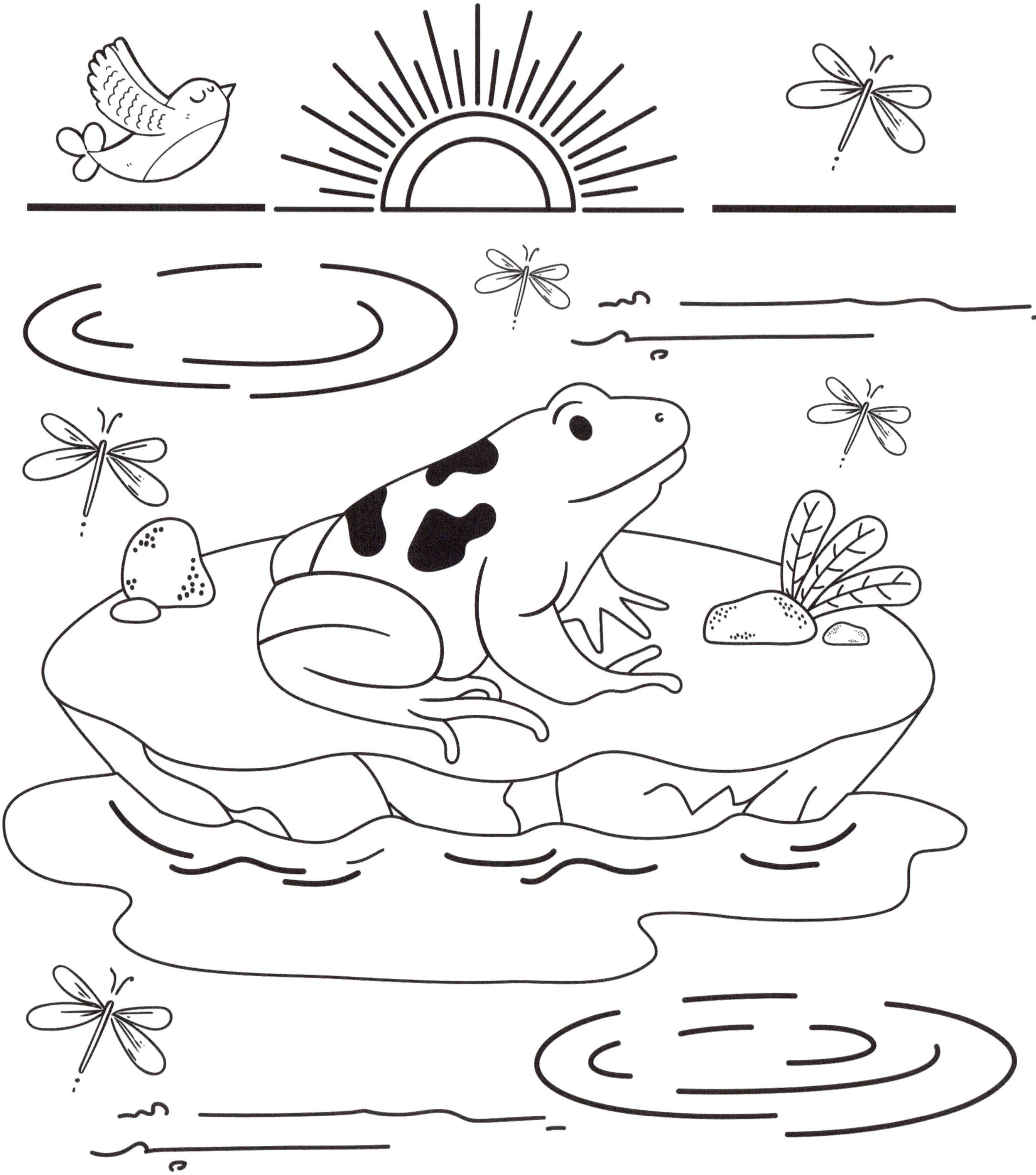

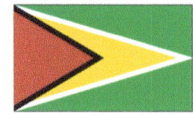

Anomaloglossus beebei (Frog)
Anomaloglossus beebei (common names: **Beebe's rocket frog, golden rocket frog**) is a species of frog in the family Aromobatidae. It is endemic to Guyana and only found on the Kaieteur Plateau, in the eastern edge of them Pacaraima Mountains. Recently, it has also been found on Mount Ayanganna.

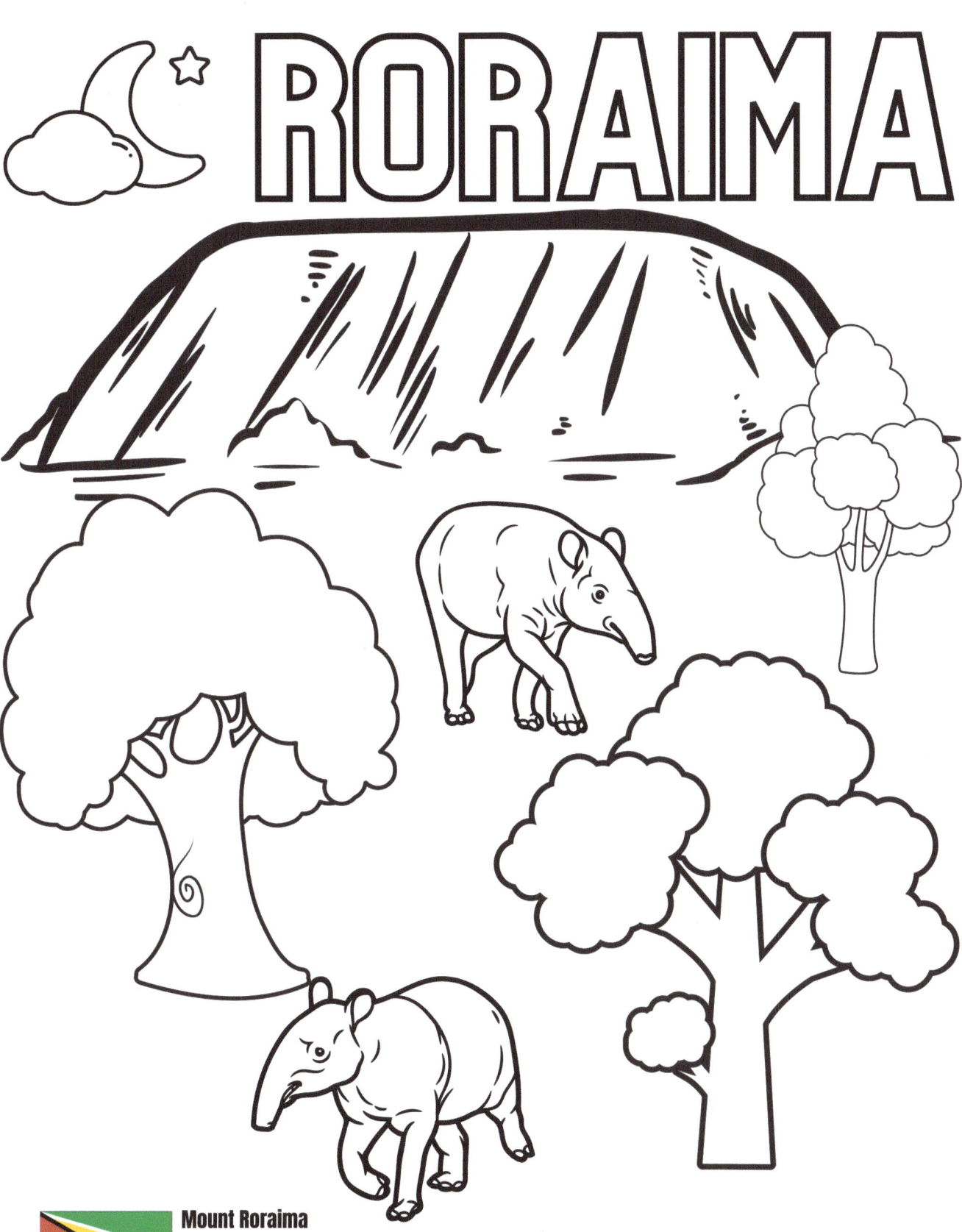

Mount Roraima
Mount Roraima is the highest of the Pakaraima chain of tepuis or plateaux in South America. It is located at the junction of Venezuela, Brazil and Guyana. A characteristic large flat-topped mountain surrounded by cliffs 400 to 1,000 meters high.

PALE-THROATED SLOTH

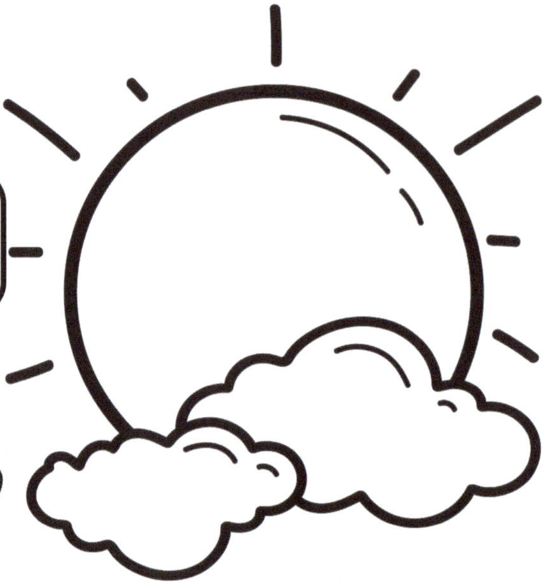

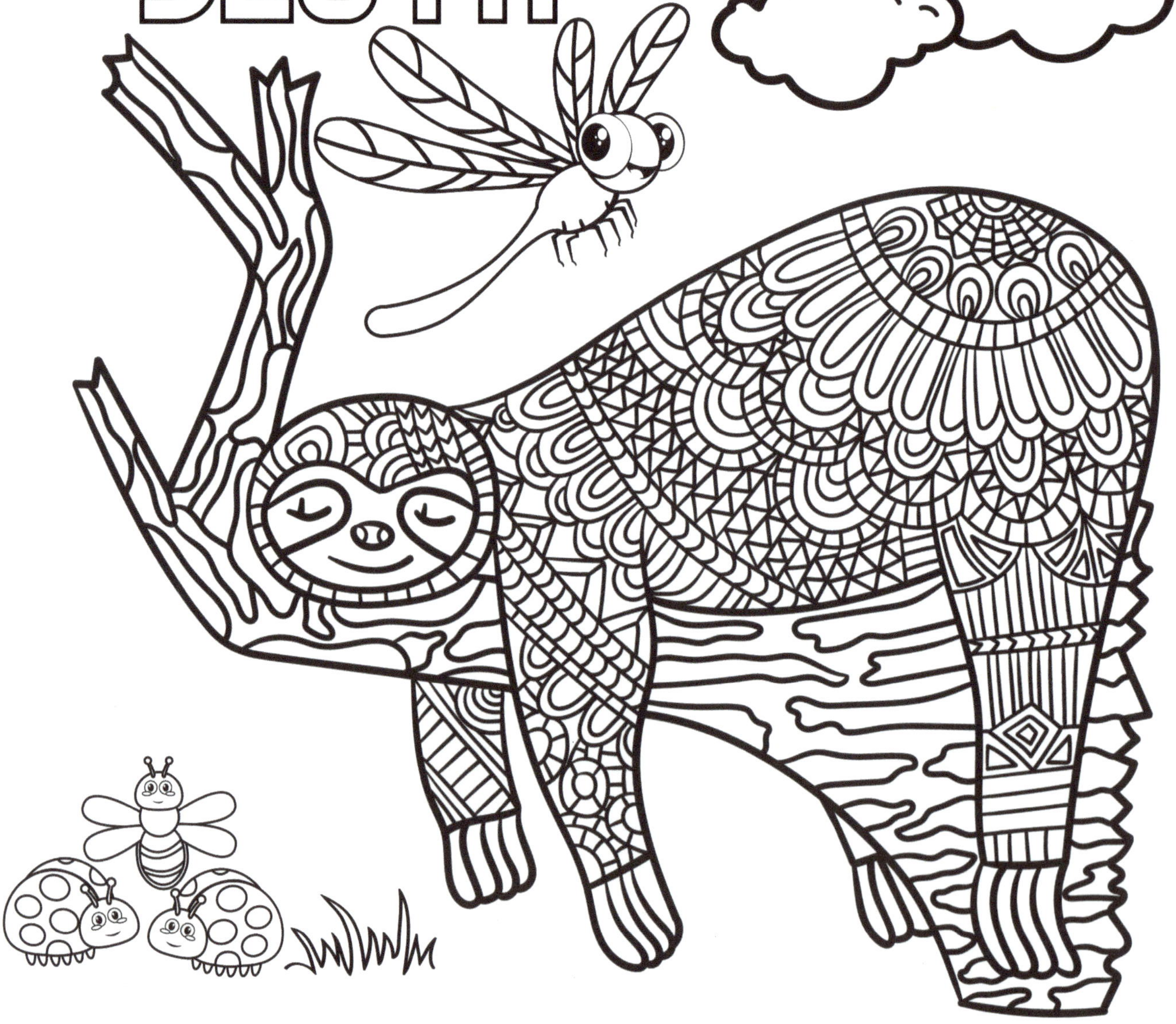

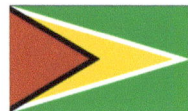

Pale-Throated Sloth

This species of a sloth found in Guyana is the pale-throated sloth. The pale-throated sloth is similar in appearance to, and often confused with, the brown-throated sloth, which has a much wider distribution. Pale-throated sloths are solitary, herbivorous animals that spend almost their entire lives in trees.

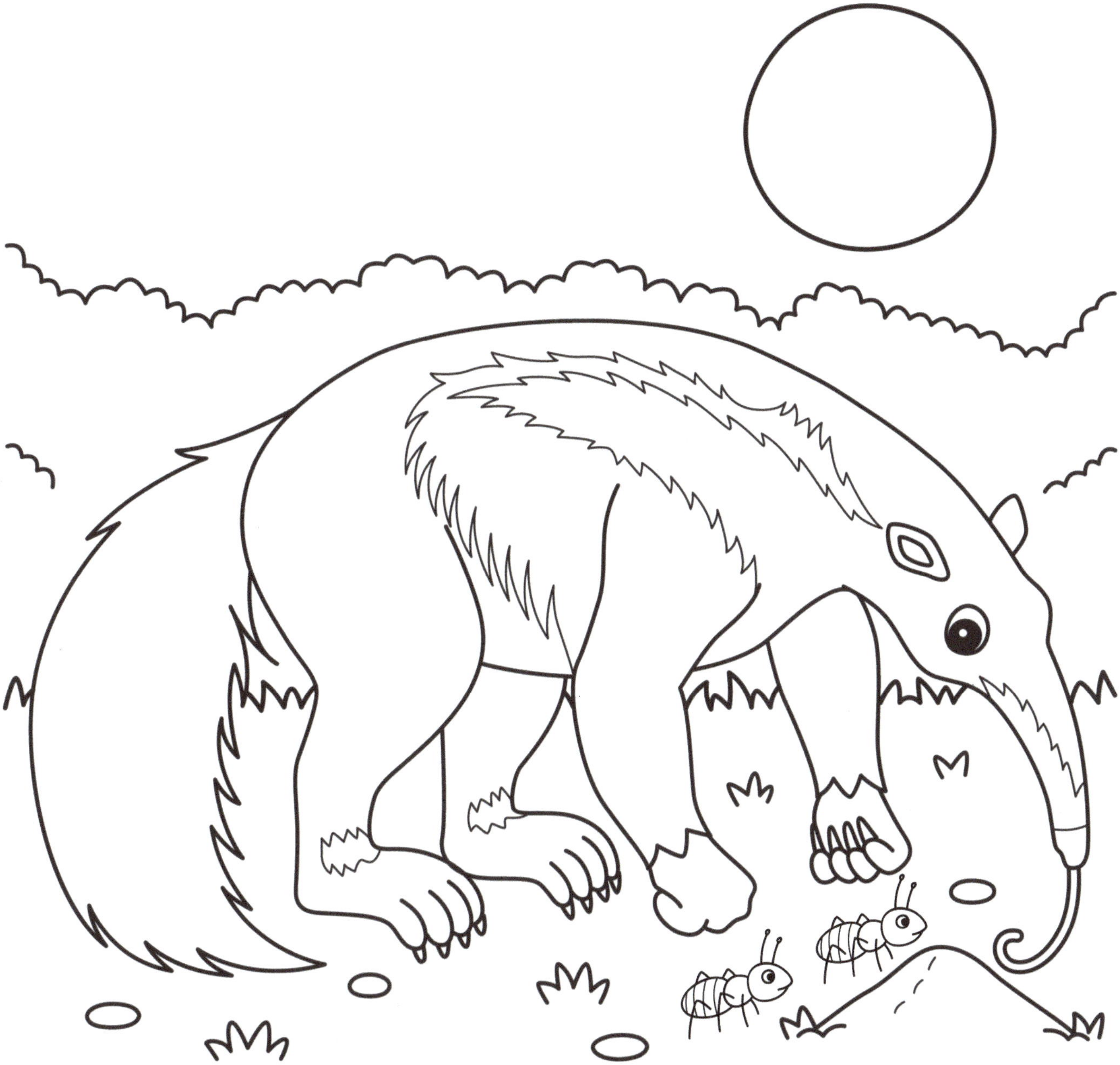

MYRMECOPHAGA ANTEATER

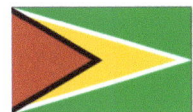

Myrmecophaga
The giant anteater is called 'Tamnuwa'. Whether it's early in the morning or late in the afternoon, these giant anteaters can be seen roaming the grasslands and forest looking for termite castles and ant hills, in the savannahs of the Rupununi, Guyana.

Thank You

THESE IMAGES WERE CREATED TO HIGHLIGHT THE BEAUTIFUL HISTORY AND CULTURE OF GUYANA. SHOWCASING GUYANA'S LANDMARKS, WILD LIFE, SPORTS, AND CELEBRITIES THAT PAVED THE WAY FOR THE COUNTRY AND FUTURE GENERATION.

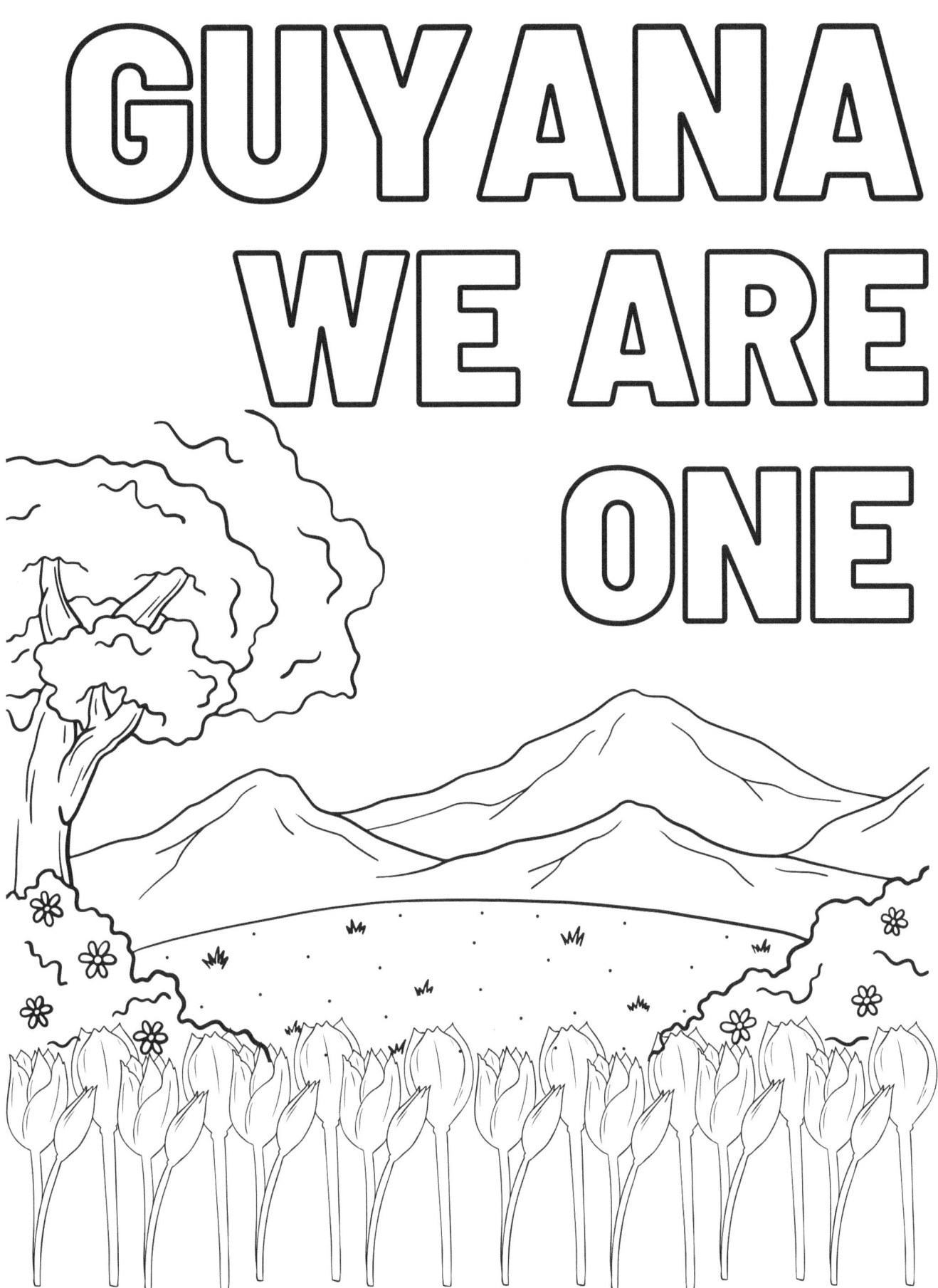

www.ingramcontent.com/pod-product-compliance
Lightning Source LLC
Chambersburg PA
CBHW040452220526
45473CB00004B/1611